ECHOES OF SINAI

Harold S. Kushner is best known as the author of *When Bad Things Happen to Good People*. He served as rabbi laureate of Temple Israel in Natick, Massachusetts for over twenty-five years. This is his fourteenth book.

ECHOES OF SINAI

Favorite Sermons of Rabbi Harold Kushner

HAROLD S. KUSHNER

TABLE OF CONTENTS

GIVING GOD THE BENEFIT
OF THE DOUBT

If we are going to be serious about a High Holy Day service and not just show up and wait for it to be over, there is a question we need to ask ourselves before we can recite any of the Rosh Hashanah prayers. The question is: Can we honestly look at this world and say that this is God's world? Can we listen to the news every morning with so much of it bad—war in one place, senseless violence in another—and come to shul on Rosh Hashanah, open our prayer books and recite a hundred or more times, "Praised are You, O Lord our God, Sovereign of the Universe ..."? Or are we just going through the motions, pretending we mean those words so that we can go home after the service and say to ourselves, "I'm glad that's over for another year"? How can we affirm the sovereignty of God in this world without having to ignore all the terrible things that are wrong with it? Is there an alternative to believing either that God wants all these things to happen or that He is powerless to prevent them?

Earlier this year, I was trying to finish my most recent book, and I wanted to say something that would take note of the new tendency to speak of the United States no longer as Judeo-Christian nation (it took us long enough to get to that point), but as "the heirs of the Abrahamic tradition," recognizing Muslims as well as Jews and Christians as having a religious presence here.

To get a sense of what the "Abrahamic tradition" was all about, I consulted the recent book *Inventing Abraham* by a biblical scholar whom I think a lot of, Professor Jon Levenson of Harvard. He suggests that Jews, Christians, and Muslims all hark back to Genesis to base themselves on God's promise to Abraham, but each of those faiths, when they read Genesis, finds a different Abraham there. Christians look to Abraham as an example of belief in God. Abraham taught that God is God and all other gods are false. So to be a Christian means to believe in God to the exclusion of any other deity.

For Muslims, Abraham is the paragon of obedience. The story we read on Rosh HaShanah is more prominent in Muslim theology than in Judaism. God tells Abraham to sacrifice his beloved son (Isaac in the Jewish version, Ishmael in the Quran), and Abraham unhesitatingly agrees to do it. So to be a good Muslim is to obey. The name "Islam" means "surrender, obedience." When Ramadan, the season of fasting, comes in June, as it did this year, whoever you are, even professional athletes and investment bankers, you fast every day from 5:00 in the morning until 8:30 at night.

Jews see Abraham primarily not as a denier of idolatry, not as a paragon of obedience. We see him as an ancestor, the founder of a people who will play a special role in God's plan for humanity. What are God's first works to Abraham in the Torah? "I will make of you a great nation...and all the families of the earth shall bless themselves by you."

I knew even before reading Levenson that Judaism, Christianity, and Islam all traced their inspiration back to Abraham, but what I did not know until Levenson pointed it out was that all three base themselves on the same verse in Genesis; they just interpret it differently.

The verse is Genesis 15:6. The Hebrew reads "*v'hu he'emin badonai*": Abraham did something to demonstrate his faith in God, and God credited it to him as an act of faith. But what was it he did? The Hebrew is maddeningly ambiguous, though it seems to have something to do with believing. Christianity sees it as theological correctness affirming that God is real and denying all other pretenders to divinity. The essence of Christian faith thus becomes a matter of believing that God exists, and living your life differently in the light of that belief. To Christians, that's what that verse means.

For Islam, to believe in God doesn't mean affirming His existence. It means recognizing and accepting God's authority, God's right to tell you how to run your life.

Jewish translations, especially the more recent ones, tend to use the word "trust." Abraham trusted God. He trusted God to keep His promise to make him the ancestor of a great nation that would teach the world about God.

I read that sentence about how Jewish translators and commentators render that key verb as "Abraham trusted God," and I remember thinking to myself, "That's it!

That's the first interpretation I've ever read that makes sense of the story we read on Rosh HaShanah." God commands Abraham to offer his son Isaac as a sacrifice and, Abraham, ostensibly, is willing to do so. Why was Abraham prepared to go ahead with such a horrible request? Because he trusted God to keep His promise to make Isaac the ancestor of a great nation. Abraham relied on God to intervene at the last moment and call off the sacrifice so that God's prediction about Isaac could be fulfilled. And that of course is precisely what happened.

Abraham was like the trapeze artist who has to trust completely in her partner. If she ever takes her mind off what she is doing for one second to check that her partner is doing his part correctly, she could fall to her death.

That's what it means for a Jew to have faith in God despite everything that is wrong with the world. Faith in God doesn't mean the certainty that God exists, and it doesn't mean that we have to accept everything that happens as God's will. Faith in God means giving God the benefit of the doubt. It demands of us what I call a "theology of not-yet." Yes, there are problems in the world—war and crime and selfishness and racial and religious hatred. They exist, not because God wants them to be there and not because God is powerless to stop them, but because God's wishes for the world have yet to be played out over time. God's powers of goodness and justice have to be channeled into human action. God doesn't change things to make the world better. People change things because God inspires them to, and people haven't gotten that message yet. In a theology of not-yet, to have faith in God means to believe that what should be, one day will be, and if it hasn't happened yet, the fault is not with God. It's with human beings for not realizing that it's up to us to make it happen.

Had you been living in Spain in the fifteenth century, at a time when Spain was the most powerful nation in Europe, you would have had to deal with the Inquisition as an expression of religious and political authority, with people being executed, burned at stake for "wrong belief." And you might well have asked yourself, "Is this what religion stands for? Torture and death threats? Isn't religion supposed to be about cultivating the divine attributes of kindness and reverence for life?" And the answer would have been, "Yes, absolutely," but people haven't come to understand that yet. In time, people will come to recognize that forced religion can never be genuine religion, but it will take time for people to grow up and understand that. The human mind evolved slowly until it outgrew its approval of torturing people in the name of God. Even today, we see crimes committed in the name of religion by people who have not yet come to understand that their behavior is the very opposite of genuine religion.

Will they ever learn? Will the jihadists one day realize that what they do in the name of Allah desecrates the name of Allah? Will racial and religious bigots who go to church every Sunday one day open their eyes and understand that what they do is not only a crime but a sin against God? I absolutely believe they will. My affirmation of a theology of not-yet assures me that one day they will, and I look forward to that day.

Had you been living in Europe in one of the countries occupied by the Nazis in the 1940s, and had to witness the murders, torture, concentration camps, and other violations of the most basic norms of human behavior, you might well have wondered, "For how long is the civilized world going to tolerate this kind of behavior? Does might make right? Does it give people the right to do such things to one another?" Ultimately, the civilized world work up to the enormity of the Nazi threat, assembling the mightiest military effort the world had ever seen to defeat Adolf Hitler. But before they came to understand the need for that, millions of innocent people suffered and died. In 1939, people *did not yet* recognize the enormity of Hitler's evil. By 1942, they were mobilized to put an end to it.

I was born in 1935. When I was growing up, my parents lived in daily dread of the childhood diseases that threatened to affect my life and health—mumps, measles, chickenpox, polio—and I am sure they were not the only ones who asked, "What kind of God would permit this to happen to innocent children in His world?" But my generation saw medical researchers refuse to accept the idea that those plagues had to be part of life just because they had been part of life for as long as anyone could remember, and one by one we learned to treat, and then to prevent, those ailments. That is what a theology of not-yet means, the refusal to see what is wrong with the world as reflecting God's will and the recognition that human action is required to do something about it.

During the years when I was a pulpit rabbi, I had a good idea of what could go wrong in God's world. I would visit people in hospitals. I would officiate at funerals. I would hold the hands of grieving widows, grieving sons and daughters. For personal as well as professional reasons, I had an idea of how much undeserved pain and anguish there was in God's world. And there were days, more than one or two, when I would ask myself, "Can I plausibly tell people that this is the world God had in mind when He created it?" The best answer I could come up with was "Not yet."

Today literacy is virtually universal. Today education is widely available. Today medicine can do remarkable things, up to and including the use of prosthetics and implants. People are living longer, and they are not spending those additional years in hospitals or in doctors' waiting rooms, as we once feared they might. Not long ago, I was invited to speak to a gathering of nonagenarians at a nearby senior living center. You had to be at least ninety years old to be part of the group, and I was delighted to see a member of Temple Israel in the group. There were about a hundred people in the audience, and when I finished speaking, they asked some very perceptive questions. Once upon a time, not that long ago, the wish that a child would grow up into his or her nineties would have sounded like a fantasy, if not an outright curse, a prediction of years of feeble confinement. But the attitude of "that's just not possible" has evolved into an attitude of "not yet" and then into a common reality.

My friend, God's gift to Abraham was the promise that his descendants would change the world, that they would teach humanity what it means to live very day in

7

the presence of God, and we've done that. Abraham's reciprocal gift to God was that he believed Him and worked to make it happen. In spite of everything that argued to the contrary three thousand years ago, Abraham gave God the benefit of the doubt. That is what I take that verse in Genesis to mean.

And because we, Abraham's descendants, were willing to assume an attitude of "not yet" rather than "not possible," we made a lot of those changes happen and we continue to work to bring the rest of it into reality. The world is still not the world God intended it to be. Some humans have made it significantly better, while others have made it worse. But to believe in God, to come to synagogue on Rosh HaShanah to affirm that faith, means to believe that we have the God-given power to make that which should be into a reality, and we make God real in this world as we do so.

TO BE AN AUTHENTIC
HUMAN BEING

Rather than focus my choice of the sermon topic on *your* problems—theological problems, family issues, wherever I thought the wisdom of the Jewish tradition might be helpful—I want to talk about one of my problems, or more specifically, the problem of being a Conservative Jew in the twenty-first century. This sermon is largely a reworking of the keynote address I gave at the centennial convention of the United Synagogue, at which I received the Lifetime Achievement Award for services to the Conservative movement. What I'm going to say this morning is not necessarily the official policy of Temple Israel, of the United Synagogue, or of anyone other than myself. It's my prescription for what it would mean to be a serious Conservative Jew and live a meaningful Jewish life in twenty-first century America.

When I was growing up in the 1940s and 1950s, Conservative Judaism was the default choice of American Jews. A Conservative synagogue was invariably the largest synagogue in virtually any city. When the move to the suburbs began after the war, the first synagogue to establish itself would be the Conservative shul. It would be an acceptable middle-of-the-road choice for all the Jewish families moving to town and looking for other Jewish families.

That was then. By the end of the twentieth century and into the early years of the twenty-first, things changed. Children of Conservative families joined Reform temples, some because they had long given up as meaningless the rituals they had been taught, some because it seemed more inviting for interfaith couples. Some graduates of Solomon Schechter Day Schools and alumni of Camp Ramah were attracted to Orthodox shuls because services there struck them as more authentic, more participatory than the bar mitzvah-centered Shabbat services of the synagogues in which they had grown up. What has happened to Conservative Judaism that we are no longer what we were for so many years, the first choice of American Jews looking for a synagogue?

My analysis of the problem begins with the observation that there are two Conservative Judaisms, two movements on the American scene competing for the right to call themselves Conservative. The first is the Conservative Judaism of the Academy, the approach to Jewish tradition that I and hundreds of others were taught at the Jewish Theological Seminary. Its fundamental premise is that there is a genius to Jewish traditional law that enables it to change as circumstances change. Jewish law evolves so that it can guide us to respond to problems Jews had never faced before, without compromising our basic values. In this perspective,

Jewish law is still seen as the will of God, its demands are to be obeyed, but it grows and changes so that those demands are always relevant, even as you are the same person you were ten or twenty years ago despite the fact that so much about you has changed. My teachers at rabbinical school taught me: "These are Judaism's answers to the challenges of life. If the questions your congregants bring you don't fit these answers, your job is to teach them to ask more appropriate questions."

That's the Conservative Judaism of the Academy, the official definition. But then, there is a second movement among American Jews that also calls itself Conservative Judaism, and it is very different from the Conservative Judaism of the Academy. It has no school that promulgates it, no official body that speaks for it, but it represents more American Jews than any other school of thought. I call it the Conservative Judaism of the community.

This Conservative Judaism was not fashioned by scholars and theologians. It was created by hundreds of thousands of East European Jews who got off the boat at Ellis Island and somehow intuited that America offered them something that no European country had ever offered, the invitation to be full citizens and participate in American life with their Jewishness not preventing them from doing so. And they said, "We want this. We want what America is offering us—the freedom, the openness, the possibilities. And they are telling us we can have it without having to give up our Jewishness."

Where Reform Jews were saying, "We want to be undiluted Americans, to do the things that other

Americans do, and we will make room for Judaism only where it doesn't get in the way of that"; where Orthodox Jews were saying, "We want to live fully Jewish lives without compromise and we will share in the American way of life only where it does not conflict with that"; the Jews of Ellis Island said, "We want both. We want to be fully Jewish and fully American, and if that means having to make a hundred compromises a day one way or the other, we would rather do that than give up either of these lives, as Americans or as Jews, because both are so meaningful and so precious to us."

Let me give you my all-time favorite example of how that worked. When I was growing up in Brooklyn in the 1940s, my family and I were active members of the Brooklyn Jewish Center, a large, very traditional right-wing Conservative synagogue. October 1, 1994: the High Holy Days came late that year. Yom Kippur was on Sunday night, October 1, and Monday, October 2, and because it was October, the sun set early and Kol Nidre was scheduled for 5:00, with most people starting to arrive at 4:30.

Sunday, October 1, 1949, was also the last day of the baseball season, and in the other religion of the Jews of Brooklyn—the worship of the Brooklyn Dodgers—the Dodgers were fighting for the National League pennant. They held a one-game lead on the last day of the season and had to beat Philadelphia to get into the World Series. (You realize I may have trouble remembering where I left my car in the supermarket parking lot nowadays, but I remember the 1949 pennant race.) At 5:00, when Yom Kippur services got under way, the game was still going on and the score was tied. By 7:30 when services were over in this very traditional right-wing synagogue in an age without cell phones, somehow everyone in shul knew how the game had come out. (The Dodgers won.) To this day, I don't understand how that happened, but to me, that has always captured the essence of what it means to be a Conservative Jew: fully Jewish, fully American, and somehow we'll work out the conflict.

I suspect my teachers at the Seminary would not have been happy with that compromise, or with some of the other compromises Conservative Jews were making back then. The official policy of the Seminary was that, if distance or illness made it hard for you to walk to temple on Shabbat, you were permitted to drive *to the nearest synagogue* but nowhere else. But alongside that official policy, tens of thousands of people who thought of themselves as loyal Conservative Jews were not only driving to shul, they were visiting friends, enjoying Shabbat in what they felt was a legitimate fashioning of a day of rest. They were saying, "I love going to shul on Shabbat, but if one Saturday I choose to drive forty miles for my grandmother's eightieth birthday party, I want to know I'm not committing a sin."

You can see where this is heading. As the Ellis Island immigrants had children and then grandchildren with no memories of traditional Jewish communal life in Europe, the gap between the most that the average Conservative congregant was prepared to do and the least that the official policy of the Academy could accept grew ever wider. The official Conservative Judaism of the Academy was a "command" theology: this is what God has told us to do and therefore this is what you should do. But fewer and fewer Conservative Jews were prepared to obey, especially if obedience created barriers between them and full participation in American life.

What I want to do this morning is to give you a different perspective on incorporating the mitzvoth of traditional Judaism into your life, doing things Jews have traditionally done but doing them not to please God or avoid offending God but rather in the service of becoming authentic human beings. It's not just about being better Jews; it's about committing yourself to Jewish observance in the name of experiencing your humanity more fully.

There is a verse in the Book of Leviticus that is translated differently in Jewish and Christians Bibles, and the difference in translation says a lot about the two traditions and their attitudes to how one should live in the sight of God. The verse is about fasting on Yom Kippur, and the Hebrew reads "*v'initem et nafshoteichem.*" The King James Bible takes that to mean "you shall afflict your souls"—that is, Yom Kippur is a day of punishing yourself, depriving yourself of everything pleasurable (food, sexual intimacy, and so on) to make up for all the self-indulgence of the past year. But listen to how the same verse is rendered in contemporary Jewish translations: "you shall practice self-restraint." We aren't asked to fast on Yom Kippur because food and sex represent the sin of giving in to gross physical desires. We do it as an affirmation of our humanity.

The goal of an observant Jewish life is to live as an authentic human being, and the essence of what it means to be an authentic human being can be summarized in four words: impose choice on instinct. That is something no other living creature can do, to impose choice on instinct: to be capable of doing something, to be tempted to do something and *choose* not to do it. Animals are totally ruled by instinct. Their instincts tell them what to eat, when to sleep, when and with whom to mate. For human beings, and this is the essence of our being human and not just another one of God's creatures, those things become matters of choice. Let me give you some examples of how that works.

Do you remember the game they used to play on Sesame Street, "Which one of these things is not like the others?" All right, which one of these four things is different from the other three: a day, a week, a month, a year? The answer: a week. The other three are all natural phenomena. Days, months, years are defined by the relative relationships of the earth, the sun and the moon. A day would be just as long, a month would be just as long even if there weren't a single human being on earth to keep track of them. But a week is a human invention. There is no such thing as a week in nature. As such, it represents the unique human ability to impose our pattern on time. That's why Shabbat is holy, because it represents our imposing our will on time, rather than time doing that to us as it does to every other creature on this planet. No other creature can do what we are doing here today, taking a day and saying it is special because we choose to make it special.

You know this. You wake up one morning and it feels like just any other morning until you remember it's your birthday or it's your wedding anniversary, and suddenly the day feels different. And should you forget that it's your anniversary, if you treat it like just another day to you, that's all right too—as long as you don't mind eating peanut butter sandwiches for supper for a week. That's what we're doing here today, isn't it? We're taking what would otherwise be just another day and we're deciding to make this a day of supreme holiness, and by our doing it, by the simple act of our deciding that, we make it happen. That's the reward for making Shabbat special in your home and family. It's not that we need the rest. It's that we are changed by that sense of empowerment, the power to work magic with time, to take the ordinary and make it special.

That, I am convinced, is what is behind the dietary laws, the system of keeping kosher. It's not because pork products are unhealthy. They may be, they may not be. That's totally beside the point. It's not because we learned that certain foods don't do well in the heat of the Sinai desert. Keeping kosher is a way of doing something that no other living creature can do. Animals instinctively know what is alright for them to eat, and when they have access to it, they will eat as much of it as they can. Their instincts tell them to do that. But we proclaim our humanity, we infuse our eating with holiness, when we impose choice on instinct. We can choose to be vegetarians, we can choose to let the values of Jewish tradition direct our food choices, and when we do so, we are eating as only human beings can eat.

Some years ago, Suzette and I were vacationing in Florida. We had to drive from where we were staying, near Boca Raton, to Vero Beach, where I had been invited to speak at a local church. Before we left, we had lunch with friends at a kosher deli in Boca, where we could eat anything that appealed to us on the menu. From there, we drove north to Vero Beach, where our hosts invited us for dinner at a local restaurant. Before we ordered dinner, we checked to be sure the soup had no chicken stock in it, and we asked that the fish be broiled plain; we had a lovely dinner and we were much more aware of the fact that we kept kosher in the non-kosher restaurant, we had more of a feeling of eating mindfully than we did at the kosher deli. We realized that we were making moral and not only taste choices, because at the restaurant we were ruled by something more than our appetites. We had to say No to certain foods. When you do that, you discover that there can be holiness and not only nourishment in your breakfast, lunch, and dinner.

There is one other ability that we have because we are human, something other animals don't have, and that is the power of speech. There, too, we can sanctify that unique gift by the way we use it and by overcoming the temptation to use it destructively. We can use words in a way no other living creature can: to console, to encourage, to show appreciation, and when we do so, even ordinary words become holy. To say "I'm sorry," to say "I'm here for you," to say "I love you," those are words that effect changes.

Now, I want to be very clear on one point. What I am offering you this morning is not what we used to call in Monopoly games a "Get out of jail free" card.

I don't want anyone going home and saying, "Rabbi Kushner says we don't have to keep the commandments if we don't feel like it because they are not really something God commanded." No, I believe the traditional system of mitzvoth, of sacred deeds, is divinely inspired, in the sense that no human mind could have come up with it unaided. But I don't believe that God dictated them verbatim to Moses and that He is disappointed in us if we violate them. What I want you to say is "I never thought of it that way before, but it sounds like something I should try." What I am offering you today, what Conservative Judaism as I understand it offers you, is the opportunity to add something very rare and special to your life, the daily experience of holiness, the profound sense of having met God in your life not only in special moments—the birth of a child, recovery from illness—but regularly, several times a day. You don't have to be a spiritually gifted person to do it and you don't have to come to a synagogue to find it. Some people never have that experience, or if they do, they don't recognize it. But when you practice Judaism as I am recommending, not as obedience to commands you don't understand and not as gesture to a vaguely remembered past, but as a way of experiencing the presence of God, a fulfillment of the biblical precept *Kedoshim tihyu*, "you shall be holy even as I the Lord your God am Holy"; when you learn to turn every meal into a religious moment, when you form the habit of seeing every person you meet, the important and the less important, the attractive and the less attractive, the familiar and the stranger—all of them bearers of the image of God; when you come to feel the power you have to take an ordinary day and make it special, so that you feel entitled to say "*Baruch Attah Adonai*, Praised are You, O God," not as a mumbled rote formula but as an authentic response to an authentically profound experience; then every day becomes a holy day, then every place you find yourself in becomes the Holy of Holies, and then everyone you meet is recognized as an embodiment of the presence of God.

The Future Can Change
the Past

In six weeks, each of us will be given the opportunity to do something we have often wanted to do. For many of us, it will be something that we have prayed for the chance to do, something we thought would make our lives significantly happier. In six weeks, we will be invited to do something about which we have often said, "If I could only do that, it would mean so much to me." And almost without exception, virtually every one of us will ignore the opportunity. Do you have any idea what I'm talking about?

As Saturday night, November 3rd becomes Sunday morning, November 4th, we will change from daylight savings to standard time. We will move the clock back and have the extraordinary opportunity to live one hour of our lives over again. And most of us will sleep right through it. What a waste of an extraordinary opportunity.

What do you think it would be worth to people who embarrassed themselves, perhaps ruined their reputations, to be able to live one hour of their lives over again and do it differently? Or for any number of politicians or public figures who saw their careers damaged by words they wish they had not spoken, things they wish they had not done, what would they give for the chance to go back in time and have a chance to do it again and do it right this time?

And what about the rest of us? Isn't Yom Kippur a time to contemplate moments in our lives when we wish we could go back and do things differently, addressing words we spoke that we wish we could recall, words we withheld that we now wish we had uttered, things we didn't do that in retrospect we wish we had done? But of course that is in the realm of fantasy or science fiction.

Or is it? It is the audacious claim of Yom Kippur that we can use the future to change the past. Rav Yosef Soloveitchik, for many years the dean of modern Orthodox Judaism, explains it this way in one of his essays: In all other civilizations, time flows from yesterday to today to tomorrow. The past determines the present, and the present determines the future. Cause and effect; something happened yesterday or last year or ten years ago, and because of that, something will happen today, and that something today will cause something to happen tomorrow. The past determines the future.

But in Judaism, Rav Soloveitchik insists, it is the future that determines the present and defines the meaning of the past. Was something a tragedy that destroys faith or was it a spur to growth that strengthens faith? Was something a mistake or was it a learning experience? We can't answer those questions solely by looking at what happened. We can only understand yesterday in the light of what we choose to do about it today and tomorrow.

Where Sigmund Freud taught that we are shaped by our childhood experiences, Soloveitchik taught that we are shaped by our vision of the future and that by choosing our future, we go back and define our past.

Now, obviously there is no time machine, no wormhole in the space-time continuum, that would actually enable us to travel back in time seventy-five years to pre-war Germany and prevent the Holocaust from taking place. But we can do things today and tomorrow, choices drawn from our vision of what kind of people we want to be and what kind of world we want to live in, and those choices will change the meaning of the Holocaust. They won't be able to bring our six million martyrs, back to life but they will determine the ultimate meaning that will be assigned to their lives and their deaths.

Our political and financial support for Israel today and tomorrow will ensure that the Holocaust did not cause the disappearance of the Jewish people. It led to our people's reemergence onto the stage of world history. That was not an inevitable result of the Holocaust, yesterday determining today; it happened only because people with a vision made it happen.

Our support for Jewish learning, within our families and in major centers of Jewish scholarship, will mean that Jewish learning did not disappear when Hitler invaded Poland and Lithuania. It was transplanted to this more congenial environment, not because of anything Hitler chose to do but because of what we choose to do after Hitler.

Our relationship with our non-Jewish neighbors and with oppressed minorities around the world will be one way in which our actions today decide what the long-term impact of the Holocaust will be. Will we respond with compassion for other oppressed endangered people so that the slogan "Never again!" will apply to God's children everywhere? Or will the Holocaust teach us to say, "Doors were closed for our people; why do these people deserve better?" Will the memory of the Holocaust teach us to believe "Scratch a Christian or a Muslim and you'll find an anti-Semite?" Or will we come to recognize that in today's America, the bigots and the hatemongers have been marginalized, and most people turn out to be pretty nice neighbors once we get over our initial wariness and stop scratching them?

Yet I suspect that when I raised the prospect of living an hour of your life over again, what probably came to mind was not geopolitics but a whole wagonload of personal regrets—arguments that didn't have to happen, omissions that you wish you could go back in time and fill in, chances that you wish you had taken, words you found yourself wishing you could take back seconds after you had spoken them.

And here, too, Rav Soloveitchik's insight that we are shaped today not by our memories of yesterday but by our visions of tomorrow, comes to our aid. Let me summarize his message in one sentence that, if you take it to heart, can save you dozens of hours in therapy: *You are not a prisoner of your past; you are the architect of your future.*

Let me show you how that works. A few years ago, a prominent Jewish educator died in Israel, and among the eulogies that appeared in the press, one person remembered an incident from early in her career. She was headmistress of a school in Jerusalem for orthodox girls. One day, the fourth-grade teacher came to her and said, "We've got a problem. Things are disappearing from girls' desks and lockers. At first, it was just things, pencils and hair ribbons. This week, money and articles of clothing were missing. We have a thief in the class." What did the headmistress? She called the class together and said to them, "What I'm going to say now applies to only one person in this room, but I don't know who it is, so I'm going to say it to all of you. Someone has been stealing from her classmates. We take this very seriously. If the missing articles are put on my desk by eight o'clock tomorrow morning, I will consider the matter closed. If not, I am warning the person who did this that there are two possibilities as to what will happen next, and they are both bad. Either you will continue to steal and one day you will get caught, and you will be embarrassed and you will be shamed. Or else you'll continue to steal and you won't get caught, and that will be even worse, because then every day of your life, you will have to think of yourself as a thief. Now I want you to consider this very carefully: Is what you are taking worth thinking of yourself as a thief for the rest of your life?" The articles were on her desk the following morning and the stealing ended. A ten-year-old girl decided that what she did tomorrow would be determined not by what she had done in previous days, but by her vision of what kind of person she wanted to see herself as being.

This is what I mean when I say that it is your vision of the future, not your memory of the past, that determines what you do. When you have learned the meaning of that story, you will have come to understand the central concept of Yom Kippur, the power of *teshuvah*.

Teshuvah is a hard idea to translate into English. It is usually rendered as "repentance," but that is inadequate, for that is such a gloomy, unappealing word. It has connotations of regret, self-reproach, thinking badly of yourself. We think of repentance as something that drains the joy from our lives. What is that line from Omar Khayyam? "Come fill the cup and in the fire of spring, the winter garment of repentance fling." But teshuvah is more than that. It is more than apologizing, more than saying "I'm sorry." It is certainly more than the half hearted pseudo-apology that you hear so often from public figures: "If something I said or did offended you, I apologize." That's just a way of saying that any hurt feelings are really your fault, not mine. I think I've told you about my rabbinic colleague who claims he begins the Kol Nidre service by saying, "If I have done anything in this past year that disappointed or offended any of you, you're probably just too sensitive." To say "if something I did offended you" is not really a way of saying "please forgive me." It's really a way of saying, "I forgive you for misunderstanding me."

So what is teshuvah? There is no precise word for it in English, probably because the concept doesn't exist in a culture that prefers to believe that "any misunderstanding is probably your fault more than mine." Teshuvah means more than "I'm sorry for what I did and I'll try not to do it again." It means something like "I don't like the person I was when I did that. I don't like being someone who could do such a thing, and I don't want to be that person anymore." It not only accepts responsibility for the past; it looks to the future. It points to a change in who you are, not just in what you do.

Carl Jung has written about what he calls "The shadow." What he means by that is all the parts of our personality that we are embarrassed by, the dark side of us, the habits that we wish were not there. So we put them behind us, like a shadow. We try not to face them. But like a shadow, they keep following us wherever we go. Teshuvah is the radical surgical procedure for getting rid of our shadow.

As an example of how that process works and what happens when it doesn't work, let me share with you what I think is the saddest verse in the entire Bible. It's found in a story about King David, early in his years as king. It occurs on what should have been the happiest day of his life. He had succeeded in uniting the northern and southern tribes of Israel into a single nation with him as king. He had conquered Jerusalem, which had not belonged to any one tribe, and set out to make it Israel's political and religious capital. As the centerpiece of effort, with great pomp and celebration, he arranged to bring the Ark of the Covenant, which had literally been stored in somebody's barn, to its permanent home in Jerusalem. The procession with the Ark included singing and dancing, and King David joined in the revelry with everyone else.

His wife, Queen Michal, daughter of the previous king Saul, watched all this from a window. For whatever reason, she didn't take part in the celebration. Maybe she felt left out; maybe she felt that all that dancing and jumping was beneath her dignity as the daughter of one king and the wife of another. Whatever the reason, David comes in all sweaty and exuberant, feeling wonderful about how the day went, and Michal says to him, "Well, Mr. King of Israel, you really did yourself proud out there, jumping and exposing yourself with your robe flying open in the midst of all those servant girls." The implication is "I didn't grow up on a sheep farm like you. I grew up in a palace and I know something about how kings are supposed to behave."

David is deeply hurt by her remark. Not only did it spoil his day of celebration, but it hurt him where he was most vulnerable, reminding him that he didn't become king by right of succession. He had been born a poor commoner who became king when King Saul and all of his sons died in battle, a battle that David chose to sit out. So he answers Michal, "I wasn't dancing before servant girls. I was dancing before God." But he is so hurt and so angry that he doesn't stop there. He goes on to say, "I was dancing before God who rejected your father and made me king in his place."

And then we come to the words that never fail to move me to tears, "*Ul'Michal bat Shaul lo hayah yeled ad yom motah*, Michal, daughter of Saul, never had a child to the day she died," meaning, I assume, that David and Michal never approached each other as husband and wife after that argument.

I find that so unbearably sad. Here are two people who once loved each other so much. David risked his life for her. King Saul had said to him, "You want to marry my daughter? Go out and kill a hundred Philistines single-handedly," no doubt hoping that one of those hundred would kill him first and solve both the problems of a political rival and the problem of an unwelcome son-in-law. Michal caught between the two men in her life, had chosen to deceive her father to protect the man she loved. It must have driven Saul crazy to find both his son Jonathan and his daughter siding with David against him.

What happened to all that love? One argument, one set of ill-chosen words at a moment when they were both tired and emotionally vulnerable, was enough to destroy it. David would go on from that day to collect wives, including occasionally other men's wives, in what I can only understand as a frantic effort to recapture the pure, uncomplicated love he once felt for Michal, but he never found it again. Michal lived out her days haunting the corridors of the palace, watching a succession of younger women take her place, feeling pitied by everyone who looked on her as the "unloved wife." And the saddest part of it is that it didn't have to happen that way.

When David and Michal woke up the next morning, they didn't have to let their feelings about each other be determined by what had happened the day before. They could have chosen to let their feelings toward each other be shaped by their visions of what they wanted to happen that day and the day after, architects of their future rather than prisoners of their past. They could have acted toward each other on the basis of a vision of two people who shared something special enough to be able to accommodate each other's faults and be vulnerable to the other person's ability to hurt them. But what would have had to happen for that to occur?

I don't think an apology would have been enough, especially the kind of apology that puts the burden on the other party. "You'll have to understand why I did that." "You'll have to forgive me for what I said; I was very upset." You realize, that's not an apology. That's a way of saying, "It's your job to put this relationship back together again because I couldn't help myself, and if you're going to be too stubborn to acknowledge that, whatever happens will be your fault." What David and Michal both needed at that moment was an act of genuine teshuvah, not repentance, not feeling bad about what happened; they already had that. Not even sincerely wishing it had not happened, but genuine teshuvah that reaches into the deepest part of your soul, so that you say, "I don't like the person I was when I did that and I don't ever want to be that person again." Not "I don't ever want to do that again" but "I don't ever again want to be the person who would do that." It's more than a change in behavior because, as we all know, when the same person tries to adopt new habits, new ways of doing things, the old habits keep stubbornly emerging. You know it's wrong, but just the same you reach for the bottle, you reach for the food, you reach for the lie to get out of an awkward situation, and you think badly of yourself for doing it again. What is needed is what is known in the terminology of Jewish law as becoming a *b 'riah hadashah*, a new person, and if you're a new person, then those things you are ashamed of, those things you wish you could go back in time and undo, you didn't do them. That wasn't you; that was somebody else by the same name. In the story I told you earlier about the Jerusalem girls' school, the girl who took the articles gave them back because she could not handle the thought of being a thief, and at that point she was no longer the same person who had taken them.

Now I know this sounds like playing with words: that wasn't you, it was someone else by the same name. But if you think about it for a moment, I think you'll see there is some validity to it. If a person is defined by his values and his ways of doing things, change those values, change those habits, and you really aren't the same person. You're someone new. But it's not easy.

You know how hard it is to change a bad habit. You do your best, you really mean to change, but time and again that feedback loop keeps telling you to repeat the behavior you're trying so hard to overcome. The only way to stop the cycle is to become a b 'riah hadashah, a different person, free from the prison of the past, like the New Jersey physician known as Bill W. who was so disgusted with his chronic alcoholism that he founded Alcoholics Anonymous to show others how to break free of the prison of the past. It involves saying, "I'm tired of wrestling with that particular demon," whether it's our eating or drinking habits, our personal behavior, our tendency to not always speak the truth. "I'm tired of wrestling with that particular demon because he wins too often, so I'm going to totally get rid of him." And that is why we have Yom Kippur.

If we're going to be serious about it, Yom Kippur can't just be a day of skipping lunch, sitting through a long service, and then saying to God, "OK, I did that for You; what are You going to do for me?" There are so scholars who see Yom Kippur as a rehearsal for death. We don't eat, we don't drink, we abstain from marital intimacy. The clergy, some of the congregants, even the Torah scrolls wear white, like funeral shrouds. Personally, I find that image a little too morbid. At most, I'm prepared to think of it as the kind of death that leads to a rebirth, the sacrifice of a part of our personality so that a new person can emerge. Think of Yom Kippur when for twenty-four hours we totally shut out the outside world—think of it as being like a caterpillar wrapping itself in a chrysalis and emerging a short time later as a butterfly. It takes courage. If you have been a caterpillar your whole life and there are aspects of being a caterpillar that you don't like but you've never been anything else it takes courage to commit yourself to being a butterfly. But if you are serious about this day and prepared to take it seriously, that is precisely what I can do for you. It can wear down your defenses. It can weaken the hold that habit has on you. It can liberate you from your shadow, from the parts of your past that you are embarrassed by, the things that you wish you had done differently, and let your new self emerge. It can give you the Jewish New Year as a brand-new start, no longer a prisoner of your past but the architect of your future.

On November 3rd, we change our clocks, but on the 10th of Tishri we change ourselves. My message for thirty years has been: Do it right and we will walk out of here at sunset tomorrow a new person, the person you have always wanted to be, rather than the person you have too often settled for being. You will have become the person God has wanted you to be all along, the person those who love you have wanted to you be all along, and you will have reason to thank God for the New Year and for the new life that God has given to you.

THE GOD OF SECOND
CHANCES

I begin with a question: Why are we here today? That may strike you as a strange thing to ask. We're here because today is Yom Kippur. For those of us whose lives are strongly shaped by the Jewish calendar, today is the most profoundly spiritual day of the entire year. We can't imagine not being here. For those whose lives are less dominated by the rhythms of the Jewish year, coming to shul on Yom Kippur is the least we can do to declare ourselves Jewish. My mentor, Mordecai Kaplan, used to describe that kind of behavior as "observing the Yahrzeit of our parents' religion." So I understand why we all make a point of being here on Yom Kippur. But why is Yom Kippur today, on the 10th of Tishri?

We understand why Passover comes on the first full moon of the spring, because that's the anniversary of when the Israelites left Egypt. We understand why the Shavout festival, the holiday of the giving of the Torah, comes seven weeks later, because that is the traditional date on which the Torah was given on Mount Sinai. We celebrate Purim on the 14th day of Adar because

it was on that date that the Jews of Persia were saved
from calamity. Rosh HaShanah comes on the first day
of the month of the fall because that is a much more
logical time to start a New Year than early January. But
what is special about the 10th of Tishri? What does it
commemorate?

Rather than admit that it is a holy day without a reason, the Sages employ some creative mathematics and
calculate that, after the Israelites offended God by fashioning and worshipping a Golden Calf while Moses was
still on Mount Sinai, and after God scolded them for it
and Moses had to plead on their behalf, it was on the
10th of Tishri that God was persuaded to forgive the
people. Therefore the 10th of Tishri became the great
High Holy Day of receiving forgiveness and making a
fresh start.

If you remember the biblical story of the Golden Calf,
the people get restless while Moses is on the mountaintop. Moses represents a visible symbol of God's presence
in their midst, and without him, they feel abandoned.
So they coerce the High Priest Aaron to build them a
statue of a calf (it was probably a bull) to represent the
presence of God in their midst.

Meanwhile Moses is atop Mount Sinai, where God
gives him the tablets of the Ten Commandments,
inscribed on stone by God Himself, and then Moses
starts down the mountain. He is confident that the people will be so impressed by what God has done for them,
not only freeing them from slavery but telling them how
to guide their lives in freedom, that they will be God's
faithful people forever. Halfway down the mountain, he

hears the sound of singing and celebration. He looks down and sees them worshipping the Golden Calf hours after they had promised God not to worship idols. Moses is so chagrined, so disappointed, that he throws down the tablets to the ground and they shatter.

That could have been the end of the story, and not just the story of the Golden Calf; it could have been the end of the Jewish people as a people consecrated to God. At one point, God says to them, "This is how you treat Me after all I've done for you? You want to march through the desert to the Promised Land, go ahead, but I won't be with you. You could have been a special people, a light unto the nations, but you settled for being like everybody else."

Moses has to intervene to plead the people's case before God. He reminds God that until a few weeks ago, these people had lived their whole lives in Egypt, their lives and minds shaped by the Egyptian way of doing things, a way of life in which nothing was deemed real unless you could see it and touch it. God relents and gives Israel another chance.

God invites Moses up the mountain a second time, and there he utters a verse that the Sages considered so important, it's recited six times in the course of Yom Kippur. "*Adonai, Adonai, El rahum v'hanun, erech apayim v'rav hesed v'emet.* I am the Lord God, merciful and compassionate, patient, loving and forgiving, promising My love until the last generation, forgiving transgressions and pardoning."

In plain language, God is saying, "I am not just a God of awesome power, a God who decides who should be rewarded and who should be punished. That is what human rulers do. I am a God of second chances. I understand that human beings can't be perfect. I help people so that they don't repeat next year the same mistakes they made last year. I give people the amazing ability to be somebody different next year than they were this past year. I am a God who helps people in difficulty, not by making their path smooth and easy but by holding their hand as they walk a difficult path, not by taking away their problems but by giving them qualities they didn't believe they were capable of, so that they can deal with the problems themselves. You yourself become the answer to your prayer."

And when the Israelites heard those words on the 10th of Tishri so many years ago, they realized they had not lost their connection to God after all. What they had lost was a childish notion of God, one that was never really true to begin with, and replaced it with a more realistic one, a demanding God who was also a God of forgiveness.

There is a school of thought in twentieth and twenty-first century theology that I have found helpful. It is known as "second naïveté." It goes something like this: Children are naïve. They believe what you tell them and believe it literally. They write letters to Santa Claus telling him what presents they want for Christmas, and they expect him to receive and read their letters. And children believe in a God who is a lot like Santa Claus, a God who will answer their prayers if they've been good and if they pray hard enough. When that doesn't work out, they stop believing in God and in Santa altogether.

That's the second stage, the stage of disillusionment and rejection. But if they are thoughtful and open-minded, they will outgrow that adolescent rejection and come to a second, more realistic concept of life, that is, a second more mature naïveté. They will reclaim the beliefs that meant so much to them as children, but this time, they won't take them literally. They will see them as poetic invocations of a profound reality. Santa Claus may not be real, but the idea behind the myth of Santa, the impulse to make someone you love happy by finding out what they want and giving it to them, that impulse is very real and can be very satisfying. The god of their childhood, the all-seeing all-judging God may not exist, but that does not mean there is no God. The God of second naïveté is a God they can believe in, a God of second chances.

I remember a story I heard years ago, about a husband and wife going out to celebrate their twentieth wedding anniversary with dinner at a fancy restaurant. Leaving the restaurant, they get into their car to drive home, and the wife turns to her husband and says, "What's happened to us over the years? Do you remember when we were courting, when we were first got married, we'd get into the car and we'd snuggle up next to each other and drive home holding each other? Now look how far apart we're sitting." And the husband points to the steering wheel and says, "I haven't moved."

Can you relate to that story in terms of how you feel about coming to shul? Can you remember a time when coming to shul was exciting, when it made you feel close to God. And do you ever wonder why you can't feel like that anymore? That's when God tries to tell us, "I haven't moved. I'm still the same God I always was, but you've shed some fairy-tale notions you used to believe about Me and you haven't found anything to replace them with. That's where your sense of emptiness comes from."

If we are lucky, we will give God a second chance, courtesy of second naïveté. We will find ourselves open to a more realistic concept of God, one not based on wishful thinking, not a God who controls everything and can be bribed and bargained with, but a God who gives us the qualities of the soul, the strength, and the resilience to deal with life as it really is; not a God who promises to protect and reward us for obedience, but a God who promises to be with us no matter what we do and no matter what happens to us that we may not deserve. That's how I understand the line in the Torah, in the Book of Exodus, the first time God ever speak to Moses, God tells him to go to Pharoah and insist that he let the Hebrew slaves go free. Moses asks God, "What is Your Name? In whose name am I making that demand?" And God answers, "*Ehyeh asher Ehyeh*," which I interpret to mean "I am the One who will always be with you." Someone has said, sometimes God calms the storm but sometimes God lets the storm rage and calms the frightened child. Sometimes God makes the problem go away, but more often God leaves the problem there and He gives us the strength and the resourcefulness to deal with a problem that won't go away.

The saga of the Golden Calf, God's anger at the people, Moses's intervention and God's forgiveness raise an interesting question: When something breaks, something that was precious to us, is it ever possible to put it together again so that it's as good as new? It would be nice to believe that a God of second chances would make that possible, but the reality seems to be, No, you can't. If it's broken and repaired, it will never be the same. The crack will always show. But what a God of second chances does is to make it possible that you will end up with something in its place that will be even stronger and better than the original. It's like the line attributed to Ernest Hemingway, "Sooner or later, life breaks us all, and we heal stronger at the broken places."

If you've gone through a crisis in your personal or professional life, in your marriage or family, and you've come through it, that relationship will be stronger than it was before. It will heal stronger at the broken place.

I had a friend who lived in Los Angeles until his death a few years ago. His name was Rabbi Levi Meir. He was an Orthodox rabbi and a licensed psychotherapist, and he specialized in counseling Orthodox families who came to him with their family issues. When a couple would come to him and tell him of problems in their marriage, problems with their children, he would tell them the story of Moses and the Golden Calf. He would describe how Moses was coming down from Mount Sinai carrying the tablets of the Ten Commandments written by the hand of God Himself. When Moses saw the Israelites worshipping the Golden Calf, he gave up on them. *He* gave up the hope of ever seeing them become the people he had hoped they would be. So he threw the tablets to the ground and they shattered. Then, after the people realized what a serious thing they had done,

God told Moses He was going to give Israel a second chance. He told Moses to go back up the mountain for a replacement set of tablets, and this time (this is the key to the story), God would inspire him but Moses himself would write the words on the stones.

Rabbi Meir would tell the couple he was counseling that the original tablets written by God symbolize perfection, even as God is perfect. But perfection is too much to expect of human beings. So God told Moses to fashion a replacement set, representing the will of God as crafted by a human being, subject to interpretation by other human beings. They would demand the maximum but leave room for human frailty and imperfection. And those were the tablets that have accompanied the Jewish people on their journey ever since.

Then Levi Meir would say to the couple, "When you married each other, it felt so perfect. You looked forward to the future being perfect forever. You would love each other and make each other happy every day of your lives. You would have children who would make you proud and never disappoint you. Then the first time you have a serious argument, the first time you hurt or disappoint each other, that's the crack in the first set of tablets. That's the loss of the dream of perfection. Now the challenge facing you is, Can you do what Moses did? Can you replace that dream of perfection, that dream of perpetual bliss, with a more realistic one, a vision that will make allowance for human frailty?"

If we can see our lives that way, that will be the comforting message of the 10th of Tishri, the Jewish holiday of second chances. Can we do what God told Moses to do: give yourself and give those around you permission to be human, to be less than perfect even as God gives us permission to be less than perfect? Leave behind your shattered dreams of who you dreamt of growing up to be and what you might accomplish, and learn to cherish who you have become, bearing the scars of experience that are the inevitable consequence of having lived.

Today is the anniversary of the day when God realized that, if He wants a world with people in it, it won't be a perfect world. He can't expect perfection from us. He can't expect us to be like God. It's enough to ask us to be human beings in the image of God, a combination of faith and frailty, aiming high and falling short, getting some things wonderfully right and some things terribly wrong. And on this date so many years ago, God forgave the people who built the Golden Calf. He forgave us for being imperfect human beings, and He hoped that we would learn to forgive each other for that as well.

Thirty-two hundred years ago on a hot day in the Sinai desert, our ancestors built an idol and they called it God. They tried to fashion a God they could understand, a God they could control with prayers, with sacrifices, with the bribery of good deeds. And when God said to them, "You just don't get it. After all I've done for you, you do this?" and when Moses had to intervene and the people feared that they had lost the chance of being God's people forever, it was today, on the 10th of Tishri that God relented and gave our ancestors a second chance.

That's what it means for us to start a New Year together, to start a New Year in the company of the people you love the most. It's a fresh start, a second chance. May it be for all of us, for all Israel, for people everywhere, a year of life and health, a year of growth and goodness, a year of outgrowing mistakes and learning to see the world not through the lens of what we've lost, but through the lens of what we've learned can never be taken away from us.

From We to Me

Some weeks ago, Rabbi Liben paid me the compliment of asking me to deliver the sermon at one of our first Friday night services. I chose as my topic the teachings of my mentor, Mordecai Kaplan, whom I described as the most influential and most controversial Jewish thinker of the twentieth Century. He invented the bat mitzvah, and he recast the language of some of our prayers so that people would not have to say things they were morally uncomfortable with, for which he was excommunicated by the Orthodox world and for which several of his colleagues on the Seminary faculty would leave the elevator when he got on. He challenged our traditional concept of God. He gave Conservative and Reform Jews a rationale for keeping some of the commandments without feeling obliged to keep them all. But that fall evening, I began by recalling my first hour with Mordecai Kaplan.

We entered the classroom, some thirty first-year rabbinical students, and sat down. Dr. Kaplan asked each of us to take out a sheet of paper and write down the names of the five greatest Jews of the twentieth century. So whom do you list? We all pretty much put down the same names: Einstein, Freud, Theodore Herzl, Ben-Gurion, Justice Brandeis. (This was 1955, too early to include Sandy Koufax.) When we were done, Kaplan said, "Now, next to each name, write the name of the synagogue where he davened every Sabbath." What? Freud went to shul on Shabbos? Einstein? None of them were regular synagogue goers. But they were Jews. They thought of themselves as Jews. The world saw them as Jewish. Rabbinical students considered them the greatest Jews of the century. But they did not practice their religion in the way that most Americans understood what it means to be religious: believing in God and attending worship services. They were Jews by virtue of their attachment to the Jewish people and the values of the Jewish tradition.

Dr. Kaplan had proven his point. We misunderstand Judaism if we insist on thinking about it in Christian categories: theological belief and church attendance. That is where I gained the insight that you've heard me quote over the years: A Christian defines himself as a Christian by what he believes; a Jew defines himself as a Jew by whom he belongs to. We are a people, a religious community, not just a bunch of men and women who worship the same God. And it is as a people that we learn how to sanctify time and sanctify life.

I went on that November evening to talk some more about Kaplan's unique ideas. Then as I came to the end of my talk, I reminded the congregation that I had begun by defining Mordecai Kaplan as the most influential Jewish religious thinker of the twentieth century, but we were now fifteen years into the twenty-first century, and many of today's Jews are different from the ones Kaplan knew and wrote about.

There has been a major shift, a tectonic shift in recent years in the way Americans, Jews, and gentiles alike, see themselves. I would describe it as a movement from *We* to *Me*. People are less inclined to see themselves as part of a larger group and more inclined to see themselves as individuals not bound to anyone else by anything other than their own free choice. In the world in which I grew up, a family was a unit: Parents and children, grandparents and cousins were like the fingers of a hand. Like it or not, you were stuck with one another. You couldn't declare yourself a free agent any more than one of your arms or legs could suddenly choose to do something that your brain wasn't telling it to do.

That sounds so awfully twentieth century, doesn't it, a world we may remember reading about but no longer live in. Today we see cartoons of families sitting down to dinner, we see couples in a restaurant. Are they talking to one another? Are they interacting with one another? More likely, every one of them is relating to his or her cell phone or iPad. Of all the remarkable inventions of modern technology, the one that seems to speak to the souls of today's young adults more than any other is the "selfie." You're vacationing in the Grand Tetons or in the Caribbean, and instead of taking pictures of the scenery, you're taking a picture of yourself enjoying the scenery. You're at a special event, the World Series, the Academy Awards, and you capture the moment by taking a picture of yourself. What is going on is less important than the fact that you are there for it.

There is a word that, for me and for members of my generation, meant something special, something rich in meaning, almost sacred. The word is "friend." It pointed to something we took seriously. It carried connotations of loyalty, sympathy, helpfulness. A friend was someone who would feel your pain when you hurt and share your joy when you were happy, someone whose pain and joy you would feel. A friend was someone who would drop everything and come sit with you if you were having a hard time. Today the word "friend" can be applied to anyone who is interested in sharing your Twitter messages or your Facebook page, and I can't help but feel that we have lost something precious in the exchange.

This focus on Me, on the individual, has even affected the synagogue. Coming to shul used to mean joining with others, forming a minyan, transcending your singularity by becoming part of something bigger. Today, for too many people, being in synagogue is a matter of having an individual experience, not a congregational experience, and if you want proof of that, you have it just a few inches from where you are sitting. Do you have any idea what I'm referring to? If you've been a member of Temple Israel for more than just the past few years, you may remember the High Holy Day Mahzor we used to use. It was called *Mahzor Hadash*, the New Mahzor, but you probably remember it as the black one. The creators of that prayer book were four disciples of Mordecai Kaplan, and its controlling ethos was that worship was a group experience, a time when you transcended your individuality. It was fashioned by Rabbi Jonathan Levine of Media Judaica, the publisher;

Rabbi Sidney Greenberg of Philadelphia as the overall editor, the man who really put it together; and Rabbi Irwin Groner of Detroit and myself as contributing editors, and it was very much a volume in the Kaplan spirit. You experienced Rosh Hashanah as a member of a community: lots of responsive readings, lots of hymns to be sung out loud. But for the last few years that we used it, even I as one of its editors had to admit that its time had passed. The new prayer book that you have at your seats, *Lev Shalem*, I think is a work of genius. It's the perfect prayer book for a twenty-first century congregation, and that's part of the problem. It's designed for an individual worshipper to experience privately, virtually no congregational readings but lots of beautiful, profound meditations for you to ponder alone. It's hard to imagine how it could have been done better.

And yet I miss those moments when a reading could summon each of us to transcend our individuality, to climb out of the isolation booth and be reminded of what it feels like to be part of a greater whole, those moments when the walls of the synagogue would echo the sound of five hundred or a thousand voices joined together. I miss it not because of what it says about the liturgy, but because of what it says about being a person, that the fullness of our humanity depends on our willingness to join our lives with others.

To share another of Dr. Kaplan's insights, he distinguished between what he called dependent and self-sufficient nouns. Self-sufficient nouns don't need anything else to be what they are. A chair can just be a

47

chair. It doesn't have to be somebody's chair. It doesn't have to be part of a dining room set to be a chair. It's just a chair. A spoon can just be a spoon.

But a woman can't be a wife that way. In order to be a wife, she has to be *somebody's* wife. A man can't be a father all by himself. He has to be *somebody's* father. A teacher needs to have students to be a teacher, a leader has to have followers. That's what it means to be a dependent noun.

For Dr. Kaplan, and for me as his student, a human being is a dependent noun. You can exist as *Homo sapiens.* You can eat and sleep and hold a job. But to live up to the definition of a human being, you need to be in relationships with other human beings. Those relationships bring out the latent humanity in you. You need friends, authentic friends, not just Facebook friends, to be a complete person. Your latent humanity fulfills itself when you connect with other human beings in a meaningful way.

That, I will insist, is what religion is really about. It's not about having a relationship with God. It's not about performing good deeds. The word "religion" comes from the same Latin root as the word "ligament," and it means "to bind, to connect." Religion aims to connect us to other people in order to articulate our humanity and in the process to successfully invoke the presence of God. That's what the idea of the minyan is all about, that together we can make things happen that we could never do alone.

Today's service will be a failure if it feels no different from the experience of being one of several hundred people showing up to see the same movie or hear the same lecture. There has to be some sense that the prayers, the liturgy, the chanting lift each of us out of our isolation and transform us into a congregation.

That's why paying a condolence call on a friend who has suffered a loss is a religious act and not just an act of friendship or a social obligation. Done right, it represents two souls meeting, two people together confronting their mortality and using religion to make it more bearable. When you understand this unique emphasis at the heart of Judaism, you will understand why a child's becoming bar or bat mitzvah is more than just an expensive birthday party. It signifies welcoming the youngster into the fellowship of people who share their Jewishness and share their humanity with one another, and his life becomes something greater as a result.

Dr. Kaplan went on to make one more point about dependent and self-sufficient nouns, and it was probably one of the most radical and provocative things that this most radical of religious thinkers ever said. He suggested that "God" is a dependent noun. Just as a woman can't be a wife without being somebody's wife, God can't truly be God unless He is somebody's God. He can make the sun rise and set on time, He can send the rain in its season, but that's not what

God is primarily about. God is about inspiring human beings to behave in a human way. That's why, in the very first chapter of the Torah, God creates human beings in His image, unique creatures blessed with the capacity to have a relationship with Him. If there were no human beings in the world acting compassionately and morally, God would only be God in potential, in theory. It's up to us to make God real in the world.

There is a story in the Bible that each of us, myself included, has heard or read a hundred times, and I think we have misunderstood it every time. It's the story of Adam and Eve in the Garden of Eden. Under the influence of Hellenism, that combination of Greek philosophy and Roman power, early Christianity and rabbinic second century Judaism turned that story into something it was not originally meant to be. We've gotten it wrong ever since. I don't think that's what the story is there to tell us. That's a Greek idea, not a Jewish one. I think Genesis 3 is the story of the birth of conscience, the development in those first humans of a trait that only human beings have, the ability to know the difference between Good and Bad. (That *was* the name of the fruit, if you remember. It wasn't called the fruit you're not supposed to eat; it was called the fruit of the knowledge of good and evil.) And I want to focus on one word in that story that I, and I suspect many of you, have misunderstood every single time we read that chapter. Adam and Eve hear God coming for them and they assume He is coming to punish them for doing something He had told them not to do. So they try to hide. God calls out to them, "*Ayecha?* Where are you?" which I, and I suspect most of us, have always understood to mean "Where are you hiding? What makes you think you can hide from Me?" But this past year, I was given reason to think maybe that's not what God is saying.

I read a book recently by an Israeli author, David Grossman, whose son was killed in the war in Gaza.

The central character of the book, who represents the author and is also a bereaved father, has no name. He is simply called The Man Who Keeps on Walking. He walks all over Israel, looking for his son, hoping that maybe the notice from the Army was a mistake and his son is alive and waiting for him somewhere. And as he walks, he calls out, "*Ayecha?* Where are you, my son?"

I read that and it was like a light going on in my head that made me see the Adam and Eve story in a different way. When they eat the forbidden fruit and they hear God coming for them, they feel guilty and hide, but maybe God isn't calling out to them "*Ayecha?* Where are you? You can't hide from Me to evade your punishment." Maybe God is calling to Adam and Eve "Where are you?" because He needs them. Without them, He can be the Creator of the world but He can't be God unless He is *somebody's* God, and there are no other candidates other than Adam and Eve.

If my reading of the story is correct, the Torah's message would be: God created human beings with the unique ability to know the difference between Good and Bad, because only with creatures who share that ability with Him can God have a relationship. God must have known that this unique creature would get a lot of things wrong, because the challenge of living morally is so complicated. But it would defeat God's purpose if we were to feel disqualified from a relationship with God because we weren't perfect, because we inevitably do some things wrong.

That's why, when we avoid coming into God's presence because we feel guilty, afraid of being judged, when we feel uncomfortable reciting prayers at home that invoke God's presence or when we feel uncomfortable coming to the synagogue because that is not something we do much of during the year and we worry that God will smell the hypocrisy, that's when God comes looking for us, calling out "*Ayecha*, where are you? I need you. There are all sorts of beautiful things that you and I can make happen together. Don't hide from me because you've done things you think I won't like." God says to us, and especially on Yom Kippur, "It's not news to me that human beings make mistakes, that they fall short of moral perfection." That's why we schedule Yom Kippur every year. We don't come here to grovel, to make excuses, to apologize. We come here to renew our relationship with a God who needs people like us, people who make mistakes and wish we were better, because God can't be God without people like us.

There is a right way and a wrong way to do Yom Kippur. The wrong way is what you were probably taught in Hebrew school when you were young: Yom Kippur is when we confess our sins to God and beg God to forgive us. The right way is to use this day to rediscover what it means to be a human being; to access our humanity by using this day to connect with other people; to move the needle back from Me to We; to reclaim and rediscover what it feels like to be needed by God, what it feels like to be part of something greater than your solitary self; to be a member of a people whose deeds of sanctification and generosity balance out all the things we get wrong, because somewhere there is another Jew doing what we left undone. That list of sins we confess to six times during the day on Yom Kippur is not an indictment nor is it a confession. It is an inventory of habits and shortcomings we need to outgrow: the shallowness, the selfishness. It's a lesson on where we need to improve. And God stands ready to help us do that.

This day if we do it right becomes a day on which we climb out of our obsession with ourselves, we reach out to those around us, we reach inward to connect with a God who needs us even as we need Him—a God who is not out there or up there but who is right here among us—and in the process, we are reminded who we are and, more importantly, who we might go on to be.

WHAT MAKES LIFE
WORTH LIVING?

When I was fifteen years old, I fell in love with Kohelet, the biblical book of Ecclesiastes. I loved Kohelet for the same reasons my fifteen-year-old grandson loves Jon Stewart and *The Daily Show*, for the same reasons that 15-year-olds in every generation have responded to J. D. Salinger's little book *Catcher in the Rye*, because I saw Kohelet exposing the hypocrisies of the adult world around me. He mocked the people he saw around him who were striving to become rich and famous. He said things like "I saw all that happens under the sun and found it to be futility and a chasing after wind" or "Don't weary yourself trying to become too rich or too smart for there is no value to it."

My attraction to Kohelet lasted longer and did me more good than most of my high school infatuations. When I was thirty and working toward a doctorate in Bible, 1 studied the book of Ecclesiastes again and now I found seriousness there, a clear-eyed piety I had not noticed the first time around. Now Ecclesiastes struck me as the work of a man trying to decide what was worth investing his energy in. Should it be the pursuit of wealth, of fame, of personal pleasure? That is a young man's dilemma and Kohelet recognized it.

Then the year I turned fifty and my father died, I made Kohelet the starting point of my book *When All You've Ever Wanted Isn't Enough*. Now I came to see the writer I found behind the book as an old man afraid of dying because dying would render meaningless everything he had worked so hard to accomplish. Now it was not a matter of which of his achievements would endure. It was a matter of whether *he* would endure.

I'm older now and once again I find myself drawn to Kohelet, asking myself, "What is this book about, this strange little book of the Bible that, like the magic mirror in Snow White, manages to know at every point of our lives exactly what question we need to hear?" And I realize it can do that because the question we need to hear at every stage of our lives is really the same question, and it's a question we are afraid to ask because what will we do if we can't come up with a good answer? The question is, What makes my life worth living? What gives me a reason to get up in the morning and face a new day?

It's the question life puts to the man or woman on the first steps of a career ladder. How do I balance the competing demands not just on my time but on my soul? How do I divide myself between home and work, between friends and family? What's the most important thing I can do with each day I have woken up to?

It's the challenge faced by the older man and woman who are reminded with every milestone they celebrate, with every funeral they attend, and with every instance of shortness of breath they experience that they won't be around forever: What can we invest ourselves in that will endure, that will testify to future generations that we were once here and this is what we cared about?

I remember the woman in her forties who came to see me early in my tenure as the rabbi of Temple Israel. She had called me and said she had an urgent problem she needed to talk to me about. She came into my office, sat down, looked at the floor, looked up at me, and said, "Rabbi, I don't know what's the point of my going on living. I have this terrible feeling that all the good things in my life have already happened, and I have nothing to look forward to.

"When my husband and 1 got married, it was so exciting. We were so happy with each other, and we looked forward to a long and happy life together. Now more than twenty years later, we're still committed to each other but the magic is gone. One day is just like every other day.

"When our children were born, we had dreams of how they would grow up to make us proud. It turns out that they're good kids, and I guess that's something to be grateful for, but there is nothing special about them. Average students, not good enough athletically to make the school team, not smart enough to get into the best colleges. I don't know why we should feel disappointed. There's nothing special about my husband or me either. But we had our hopes.

"My job, it's the same thing day after day, and I'm finding it harder to get up and go to work in the morning. We had dreams once, and now all we can do is hope that things don't get worse. Rabbi, I have half my life ahead of me and nothing to look forward to. What reason do I have to go on living?"

I've never forgotten that conversation. 1 don't remember what I said to her back then, but I find myself wondering what I would say to her today. If it took me most of my adult life to figure out what question Ecclesiastes was asking, and it's the same question that woman was asking—What makes life worth living?—it took me even longer to understand his answer. Listen to what he has to say at the heart of his book:

> "Go, eat your bread in gladness and drink your wine in joy, and God will approve of your actions. Let your clothes always be freshly washed and your head never lack for ointment. Enjoy happiness with the one you love all the fleeting days of life that you have been granted." (Ecclesiastes 9:7-9)

I remember reading that for the first time years ago and saying to myself, "That's it? That's the best he can come up with: Life is brief so go out and have a good time, get drunk, buy yourself a new outfit, for that is the whole of life? What kind of answer is that? What kind of biblical answer is that?"

But ultimately I realized 1 was misreading him. He wasn't saying, "Life is unsatisfying so go out and eat and drink and try to forget your problems." He was saying, "For many people, life is unsatisfying because we have forgotten how to enjoy it." We live our lives in such a narrow emotional range. No highs, no lows, we've become strangers to joy and afraid of sorrow.

We once knew how to enjoy ourselves. When we were children, there were so many things that excited us—a trip to the playground, to the beach. At birthday parties, it wasn't even the presents that made us glow with pleasure. We loved playing with the boxes the presents came in. But with time, that capacity to be excited began to fade. Children today are so emotionally overloaded that their systems shut down. I've been to birthday parties where the celebrant faced a tower of presents as tall as he or she was, and opened each one in a spirit of "that's nice; what's the next one?"

By the time we become adults, many of us have totally lost that capacity for feeling joy. Psychologists have determined that the average five-year-old laughs 300 times a day, the average adult 17 times. I have this theory that professional sports are so important to American men because it is the only place they can feel free to be emotionally open, to cheer, to groan, to dread, and sometimes to exult. Outside of the arena, the only emotion many men are comfortable displaying is anger. Even something as normal and inevitable as sorrow is seen as unmanly. In the Bible, King David is not afraid to cry at the death of a friend, but today's man sees that as a sign of weakness. That may be why so many of the conversations about politics, lifestyles, and other social issues, and even about the local sports teams, are angry ones. Anger and sadness are the only emotional notes we remember how to sound, and as a result, we live our lives entirely in tones of black and grey. What happened to things like joy, hope, longing, fear, awe, cheerfulness, compassion? They've become foreign to us.

So if one of the reasons life has lost its savor for many of us is because we live it in such a narrow emotional range, what is the cure? This happens to be one of the problems to which religion may have the answer. Religion done right can help us rediscover something we had when we were young and lost along the way, our sense of joy, of wonder; it dots the calendar with red-letter days to give us opportunities to celebrate and rejoice. It transports us from the everyday world of grey to a world of living color. Religion done right teaches us how to work through our grief when something sad happens to us rather than take a pill to hide from the pain and then realize months later that we are carrying an undigested lump of sorrow under our hearts.

We have a holiday coming up in a few days, Sukkot. Our tradition calls it *z'man simchateynu*, the season of our rejoicing. But will we rejoice? Most of us will spend those days going to work, carrying on our lives as usual. But some of us will take that opportunity to rejoice to make decorating a sukkah the Jewish equivalent of a Christian family decorating a Christmas tree. Some of us will be reminded that Sukkot was the prototype of the Pilgrim Thanksgiving and take those days as a time to celebrate the bounty of the earth, the good foods available at this season. Some of us will find a way to treat our souls to the spectacle of the leaves turning color in a New England autumn. And the rest of us will have no idea of what we're missing.

For those who ask "Why doesn't God work miracles for us the way He did for our ancestors?" I think the miracles are still there. It's not that God has changed; we have forgotten how to notice them.

When I was in college, I took a few evening classes at the Jewish Theological Seminary before I entered rabbinical school. I had a theology class with Abraham Joshua Heschel before he was famous. One evening, I remember, he came into class and said to us, "Something remarkable just happened as I was walking to class." We all perked up; what was this remarkable thing? He went on, "The sun set over the Hudson River, and nobody stopped to notice it except for a few Jews who realized it was time for the Maariv service." He went on to speak about a legacy of wonder as one of the greatest gifts of the religious tradition, something he'd later write about in one of his books. One of the most important things we can do to preserve that legacy of wonder and to preserve our feeling of closeness with God is to never take anything for granted. But today we've lost that sense of wonder. Modern science can explain why things happen and how things work, and as a result, all sorts of amazing things strike us as ordinary.

The woman who came to see me forty years ago, complaining about how pointless and empty her life was, had I been as wise then as I am now, I could have pointed out to her the miracles that sustained her life daily. Truth be told, she was not the most attractive or the most scintillating woman in the congregation, but she had a husband who loved her and was loyal to her.

And her husband wasn't the best-looking, most success-ful man in town, but she was capable of sharing her home, sharing her dinner table, sharing her bed with him. And if their children weren't top students or top athletes, they were two healthy children, unaffected by any of the hundreds of things that can go wrong with a growing child. Weren't those miracles enough to redeem a person's life from meaninglessness? And we take them for granted.

Religion done right would give us the courage to take off the armor we wear all year long to protect us from feeling. It would say to us, "Dare to love even if it doesn't work out as you hoped it would. Dare to dream even if you know that most dreams don't come true, because there is so little to life without love and without dreams, and because we are strong enough to survive disappointment, and more than that, we are too strong to have to live our lives timidly.

Where else can a person turn to find a sense of meaning and purpose in his or her life? I heard a speaker once describe the experience of stepping onto a scale and being told that he weighed 425 pounds. That seemed a bit excessive for him, so instead of heeding his first impulse and trying out for the Patriots' offen-sive line, he stepped on another scale next to the first one and found that he actually weighed only 68 pounds. That was more like it. You've probably figured out what was going on. He was at a science museum, at an exhibit of what we would weigh under the influence of gravity on other planets. Someone who weighed 180 pounds on earth would weigh 425 on Jupiter but only 68 pounds on Mars. The speaker explained that the greater the mass of the place where you find yourself standing, the more weight you will represent. He went on to make the homiletic point that if you want to feel significant in the world, if you want to be a person of consequence, you need to attach yourself to a significant cause. Devote yourself to something that really matters and immediately *you* matter, and the more significant the cause, the more significance your life will take on.

The psychiatrist Viktor Frankl broke with Freud over Freud's definition of life as the pursuit of pleasure and the minimizing of pain. Frankl defined life as the pursuit of meaning and the shunning of insignificance. Our days may be crowded but our days will be empty unless we fill them with something worth caring about, something we can feel good about devoting ourselves to. It has been said that service to others is the rent we pay for the space we take up on God's earth.

Most of us have work and families to engage us, and they usually do a good job of filling our days. But sometimes our work and our family commitments aren't enough to satisfy our need for ultimate meaning. They are like two legs of a three-legged stool, necessary but not sufficient. We need the third leg and that can be engagement in some cause beyond our own needs.

You've seen some of your neighbors take on responsibilities here at Temple Israel or in the communities you live in. Have you understood why they do it? And how often in the past year or two have you read about a successful business executive leaving his job to do something less lucrative but of more value to society? How often have you read about a famous movie star dedicating himself or herself to some worthy cause, Darfur or AIDS or world hunger? And their reasons for doing it could have come straight out of Ecclesiastes. "I worked hard for years to make money only to realize there has to be more to life than that." That explains why so many busy people, so many talented people, devote so much time to responsibilities in this congregation or to some good cause. They are saying that if you make success the sole purpose of your life, then you risk having it become the end of your life, meaning there will be no more to your life beyond that.

It doesn't have to be a world-changing cause. Our ancestors in the shtetl, the world of *Fiddler on the Roof,* didn't have the material opportunities that we have, but I suspect they never had to ask themselves, "What is the purpose of my being alive?" Whatever they may have done to make a living, or to almost make a living, if they were tailors or grocers or housepainters, they knew that their real role in life was to be God's agents on earth. The other stuff was just to pay the bills for it. They believed that by living lives of piety, holiness, and helpfulness to neighbors in need, they made God present in this world and made this a world God would tolerate. Now, there's a cause that will add substance to your life.

What makes our lives worth living? I've saved the most important part of my answer for last. Barbra Streisand has it only half right when she sings about how the luckiest people are those who need other people in *Funny Girl.* She's right that we all, and especially men, need to be warned against the sin of self-sufficiency, the idea that a real man can do it by himself without having to ask for help. My friend Deborah Tannen, who has written those marvelous books on how men and women communicate differently, once told me that she had assured herself of a place in history by figuring out why men don't ask for directions when they're driving. She summed it up in one sentence: Women's souls are nourished by relationships, men's souls are nourished by achievement. She may not have realized it, but she was paraphrasing Genesis 1. God creates Adam to work, to till the soil and care for the garden. God then creates Eve to be a companion and exercise the unique power to generate life. That's why women have an easier time asking for help. Whether it's seeing a doctor, going to a therapist, or just asking for assistance around the house, asking for help establishes a relationship and relationships are good, whereas for men, asking for help is an admission of weakness, of limited competence, and weakness is bad. That's why men are more likely to have buddies, somebody to watch a ball game with or go fishing with, and less likely to have the intense, sharing friendships that women have.

That's the part Barbra Streisand got right: it's good to realize that we need other people. But she left out the more important point: what we need to understand most is that other people need us. That is the real answer to Kohelet's question of what makes life worth living. Live because people need you. Live because God needs you to make certain things happen in His world. There is no more sustaining feeling, no more redemptive feeling than the knowledge that somebody needs you.

We don't live only for ourselves. We live for others and our lives take on unmistakable meaning and purpose when we live them for others. Dr. Sherwin Nuland, a physician who has a Jewish background and has written some really good books, tells of getting a letter from a seventy-year-old woman who asked him the question we've been pondering: "My life is essentially over, I've done all the things I'll ever do. What is the point of my going on, just to get older and sicker?" Dr. Nuland wrote back to her, "You must live for the sake of those who love you. They need not only your physical presence in their world. They need your wisdom, in ways you may not fully appreciate." He went on to say how much he would have been deprived of had his grandmother left this world when she was seventy and not been there to enjoy and enrich his life. To give up on life while you're still alive is to reject God's plan for your life.

What would I say today to that woman who sat in my office forty years ago and asked me what she had to look forward to in life? What would I say today to the person who asks me, "What do I have to live for?" The elderly person, the chronically ill person, the person without immediate family, the person whose plans for life never worked out the way he thought they would, or for that matter, the successful person who feels he has done so much already and has no more mountains to climb and no more energy to climb them? I would tell them first that if they just took off the armor they wear to protect themselves against feeling pain, they would realize how many miracles surround them, just waiting to be appreciated. I would tell them, "You're not here only for yourself, for the pleasure that life might or might not bring you. Your life connects to so many other lives. Take one piece out of the puzzle, leave one ingredient out of the recipe, and it's just not the same." I would share with them the Jewish legend that at the revelation of the Torah at Sinai, there were 600,000 Israelites standing there to receive a Torah that contained 600,000 letters and vowels. Just as, if one of those letters was missing, a Torah is not fit for public use, had one of those Israelites not been there, the Revelation would not have happened. Any one of those Israelites could have said, "What difference does it make if I'm there or not? Who'll notice?" But the legend would tell us that every one of us makes a difference. It would be a smaller, colder, emptier world without you.

At the High Holy Days season, we pray, "*zochreinu l'chaim melech hafetz b'chaim*, Remember us unto life, O God who desires life." Or maybe it means "Remind us how rewarding life can be even when it isn't perfect, and remind us of why we have come here to pray for another year of life." May the New Year find us all inscribed in the Book of Life and may we have reasons to be grateful for that.

THE STONE THAT BLOCKS
THE WELL

Just about a year ago, right after the High Holy Days, I adopted a new mitzvah. I committed myself to studying the weekly Torah portion with the commentary known as the *Sefat Emet*. *Sefat Emet* means "The Language of Truth." It was written by the prominent Hassidic leader the Gerrer Rebbe, who died just over a hundred years ago. I had heard great things about this commentary, not just from devotees of Hassidism but from people who praised him for his psychological insights in an age before Freud. As I studied it, I was impressed by the Gerrer Rebbe's ability to find messages in biblical passages that I had probably read a hundred times and thought I knew well.

For example, there is an incident in the Book of Genesis. The patriarch Jacob has to leave home in a hurry. With his mother's complicity, he has gained the blessing of his father, Isaac, designating him as the future leader of the family, by deceitful means, by disguising himself as his slightly older twin brother, Esau, and fooling his visually impaired father. He runs away to go to the home of his uncle Laban, his mother's brother, in the neighboring country of Aram.

The Torah describes how Jacob arrives in Laban's village and sees the local shepherds standing around the village well with their sheep. He asks them, "Why are you standing around and not watering your sheep?" They point to a large stone on top of the well, to keep the water from evaporating and to prevent stray objects from falling in. The stone is too heavy for one or two men to roll off; they have to wait until all the shepherds have arrived and together they move it.

Jacob asks them if they know a man named Laban in their town, to whom he is related. They answer, "Yes, we know him, and in fact, here comes his daughter Rachel with his sheep." Jacob looks at his cousin Rachel and is struck by her beauty, even though the only things he can see of her are her eyes. She apparently had very attractive eyes. Inspired by the sight of her, Jacob single-handedly rolls the stone off the well and invites the shepherds to water their sheep.

That's the story. If I read it a hundred times over the course of my career and while I was writing the commentary to *Etz Hayim*, I never saw anything to it except an account of a young man trying to impress an attractive woman he has just met. But listen to what the *Sefat Emet*, the Gerrer Rebbe, does with that story: "*Yesh b'chol davar nekudah hanotenet hayyim v'zeh be'er basadeh.*"

The well is not simply a well. It symbolizes the source of everything that makes life possible and worth living. And the stone is not just a stone. It symbolizes all the things that block our access to those life-giving waters.

Our challenge, says the *Sefat Emet*, is to do what Jacob did, to summon all of our strength and remove those stones that block the well.

What are some of the stones that we have to lift out of the way so that we can enjoy our lives as I believe we were meant to? For starters, let's begin where Yom Kippur begins, with Kol Nidre. Imagine a non-Jewish friend asking you, "What is this holiday that you all take so seriously? What is this prayer that everybody hurries through an early supper to come for?" I suspect you would say to him, "It's Yom Kippur. That's when we come to synagogue to confess our sins and ask God to forgive us" And if he is a really close friend who is comfortable saying this, he might ask, "Do you really believe that?" And if you're comfortable being honest with him, you might answer, "No, not really. I don't think the things I do are sins, and I don't believe that I need to beg God to forgive me. But it's only once a year, so I do it."

Sound familiar? Well, I have news for you. Listen to what we said in Kol Nidre: "All vows, promises, commitments and renunciations that I made between last Yom Kippur and tonight, may they be annulled, canceled out, and regarded as nonbinding."

Did you hear that? Kol Nidre is about promises, commitments, things we said we would do. It's about renunciations, things we promised we would stop doing. What is it not about? What word did you not hear in Kol Nidre? There was nothing about "sins." It's not about sins in the eyes of God. It's about things we said we would do and never got around to. It's about habits we promised we would break and we meant it when we said it, but we couldn't do it. There will be plenty of times in the course of Yom Kippur when we will beat our breast and admit our sins, but Kol Nidre, the prayer that sets the tone for the day, is not one of them. What would be a more accurate word than "sins?" How about "regrets"? The first stone that blocks our access to the well is the accumulation of regrets we feel when we look back at last year—memories of things we intended to do but never did, things we gave up on because it turned out they were harder than we anticipated, bad habits we genuinely intended to break but somehow they persisted. We feel less good about ourselves because of them.

Is there a cure for the burden of regrets? Is there a way of feeling better about ourselves, giving ourselves reason to hope that we won't keep on doing the same things we're embarrassed for doing? There is, and it's a fairly simple one. It's called "starting a New Year," putting last year behind us, turning the page, looking at a blank space in the Book of Life where we haven't done anything wrong yet.

To take an example from the world of sports: imagine a baseball team that started the year with high hopes and ended up fifteen games out of first place. The team looks back on all sorts of missed opportunities, bad breaks, decisions that didn't work out, and they feel depressed. Their only consolation is that they don't have to start next year fifteen games behind. In a New Year, we all start even, we all start with a blank slate. Last year's mistakes don't count against us. That's Kol Nidre. It's not about groveling and asking forgiveness for our sins. It's about the regrets we carry from the year gone by: all the unkept promises, all the good intentions never carried out, all the decisions in which we meant well but they didn't turn out that way. Leave them behind in the past. Let them be last year's news. Learn from them but don't be burdened by them. They don't have to be a permanent part of you. Last year is over. The regrets of Kol Nidre represent who we used to be, not necessarily who we will be. That part is up to us. Believe in your ability to be different. Summon the strength to roll away the stone of regret that blocks the well and help yourself to the fresh water.

What else comes between us and the prospect of looking forward to the New Year? I would suggest the stone of envy, feeling bad when you see other people having things you would like to have, doing things you would love to be able to do. Someone has suggested that envy is the only sin you can't enjoy while committing. Is there a cure for envy? Is there a trick to rolling the stone of envy off the well so that we can enjoy our own lives more by not comparing them to someone else's? It turns out that there is and I can teach it to you in ten words: *Focus on what you have, not on what you lack.* Think of something others would envy you for. That's all there is to it. Think of something one should envy you for.

The word for a Jew, "Yehudi," means "one who is grateful." It comes from the story of the birth of Jacob's fourth son. His mother calls him Yehudah, saying, "For this, I will thank God." What has happened to us is that American culture has messed up our minds by advertising things that claim they will make our lives happier if we had them, and we come away thinking that, since I

71

don't have them, gee, I thought I was happy but I guess I'm not. What has happened to us is that we have confused God with Santa Claus and learned to thinking of prayer as giving God a list of all the things we want but don't have, and persuading Him that we've been good girls and boys so we deserve them. I'm sorry, that's not God; that's Santa Claus. Authentic Jewish prayer knows there is no Santa Claus. Jewish prayers are all about thanking God for what we have and recognizing that we have no claim on Him for even that much, let alone everything on our wish list. That's why the author of the 23rd Psalm can say "*kosi r'vaya*, my cup runneth over," not only when things are going well for him but even when he's just made his way through the valley of the shadow of death.

And the other half of the trick to cleanse your soul of envy is this: all those people you're jealous of—you have no idea what pain they are carrying around in the privacy of their fancy homes and in the privacy of their hearts. We read about their multiple divorces, about estranged children and children in trouble with the law, about their compulsive resorting to cosmetic surgery, and it never occurs to us to ask ourselves, "Why am I envying those people?" I've spoken to them, I've read their letters to me about why they needed to read my books: their family issues, the distortion of values, the parts of their souls they realize they left behind to shrivel and die in their pursuit of success. Yes, they know that people like us envy them and they find it ironic.

Perhaps the biggest stone of all blocking our access to the well of personal fulfillment is the stone of anger.

Angry people can't enjoy their lives. Angry people find it hard to love other people. We're angry at the way parts of our lives are turning out. We're angry at people who didn't treat us right, even if it happened years ago, even if we know it may have been inadvertent or the result of smallness on their part. We blame our mates for not providing us with the happiness they said they would, we blame our children for not being the *nachas*-producing machines we had hoped for, and most of all, we blame God. We're angry at God because the world isn't a nicer, fairer place, and we blame Him for not fixing everything that's wrong with it. I think that may be the real reason people stay away from synagogue all year long and come grudgingly on the High Holy Days. It's not a critique of the singing, the sermon, or the food at the Kiddush. People don't come because they believe they have nothing they want to say to God and, as long as He is not prepared to apologize to them, God has nothing to say to them. Now, being angry at God is not necessarily a bad thing. Anger can be part of an honest relationship, as long as you care enough about the relationship to try to work through the anger.

Over the years, one question has frustrated me more than any other. It came from an involved member of the synagogue who asked me at a particularly difficult time in his life, "If God could let this happen to my family, what was the point of our coming to shul all these years?" At the time, I didn't know what to say to him. It didn't matter because he wasn't really looking for an answer. He wasn't looking for theology; he was looking for reassurance that he and his family were good people in my eyes and presumably in God's eyes as well. At the time, I answered him best by explaining less and hugging more. But the question lingered.

There were times when our family was dealing with a serious health crisis and I found it impossible to recite the line in the daily service that spoke of God as "*Rofei holei amo Yisrael*, the One who heals the sick among His people," because my personal as well as my professional experience contradicted that. God doesn't always heal the sick, the seriously ill. I finally came to understand the line to be saying not that God is capable of healing all illnesses if He wanted to; what the prayer is saying is that serious illness is a serious business. Not everyone gets over it and nobody gets over it permanently. Any time someone does, any time your body fights off a cold or heals from a wound, any time antibiotics cure an infection, any time surgery cleanses you of a tumor and you're healthy again, it's a miracle, It's a miracle precisely because it doesn't happen predictably, automatically, and when it does happen, you have experienced God in your life and you can authentically praise Him for your being the recipient of an unpredictable miracle. I came to realize that making sick people healthy is not God's job. That's the doctor's job. God's job is making sick people brave, and you know, that's something He does really well.

Think of it this way: A homeowner's insurance policy doesn't prevent your house from catching fire or being damaged by a flood. What it does is see to it that, if such a thing were to happen, you would have the resources to restore your home. A life insurance policy doesn't keep someone from dying. It assures you that, if that should come to pass, your family will have the resources to go on with their lives. And a life grounded in religious faith and practice, a life of study and synagogue attendance, won't keep bad things from happening to you. You'll still be vulnerable to the illnesses and accidents to which the flesh is heir. What it will do is provide you with the emotional resources you need to survive even the worst of circumstances.

Studies have shown that religious people are less angry than nonreligious ones. Their lives are less polluted with generalized rage, because they understand that God is on their side, that He is angry at the same things that they are—crime and sickness and suffering—and that He can be a resource for our doing something about them.

To go back to that scene in the Torah, Jacob says to the shepherds, "Why are you standing around in the hot sun? There is water right in front of you. Drink it, refresh yourselves and your flocks. You'll feel better." They answer him, "You're right. We're thirsty, our sheep are thirsty and some cold water would taste wonderful. But that large boulder is blocking our access to it. We can't move it." Jacob rolls the stone off the well and says to them, "You see, it's not as hard as you thought it was. Believe in yourselves, believe in a source of strength beyond yourselves, and you'll be surprised by what you can accomplish."

Tonight the Yom Kippur service holds a similar conversation with us. It says to us, "This world is full of blessings. Why aren't you gathering your share?" And we answer, "We don't believe we're up to it. We're not sure we deserve it. We're disappointed in ourselves, and in our ability to change and stop doing things we know are wrong. We've seen people who are stronger and smarter than we are grab all of the good things in life, and we've learned that we can't count on the world to distribute blessings evenly." And the Yom Kippur liturgy say to us, "You're giving up too easily. Like the shepherds in the Jacob story, you don't know your own strength. God is saying to you today, "I don't care if you don't believe in Me. There is nothing in tonight's service, not one line, about a requirement to believe in God. I want you to believe in yourselves. I want you to believe that you have the power to turn the page, to leave the regrets and mistakes of last year behind and start the New Year fresh. I want you to believe that you are already more blessed than you realize. Stop looking at what other people have—for all you know, they are envying you—and realize how blessed you are. And I want you to know that when you strive to make this year a New Year, a kinder year, a happier year, you won't be struggling alone. God will be at your side."

Let us begin to roll the stones off the well, the stones of regret, of envy, of rejection of religion born of anger, of everything that keeps us from enjoying all the things in the world that are waiting for us to enjoy them. And let it be our prayer that, when we gather here at this time next year, we will be looking back with satisfaction at how much we have done and how much we felt blessed in the process.

Jacob's Fears and Ours

A man came up to me one evening after one of my lectures and said to me, "Rabbi, you seem to know the Bible pretty well. Can you tell me, of all the things that God says to people in the Bible, what sentence does God repeat more often than any other?" I thought for a moment and said, "Probably the one about being kind to the widow, the stranger, and the poor person. I think God says that five or six times in the Torah." He shook his head and said, "Not even close. The sentence God repeats more than any other is: "Don't be afraid."

I checked it out when I got home and it turns out that the man was right. More than eighty times, God says "*Al Tira*, fear not," don't be afraid. He says it to Abraham, to Isaac, to Jacob. He says it to every one of the prophets and tells them to say it to the people. I believe God is trying to get that message to us today: Don't be afraid when you read the news coming out of the Middle East. Don't be afraid when you hear about the problems facing American society. It's not that there is nothing to be afraid of. There are lots of things to be afraid of, but God wants to reassure us that we can handle them if we are not paralyzed by fear.

For forty days before Yom Kippur and for ten days afterward, we add a psalm to our daily prayers every morning and evening, a psalm we don't recite at any other time of the year. It begins: "*Adonai ori v'yishi, mi-mi ira? Adonai maoz hayyai, mi efchad?* God is my light and my salvation; whom shall I fear? God is the source of my strength; of what shall I be afraid?"

Now, when the psalmist tells us three times in the first three lines that he's not afraid, the message we hear is that he *is* afraid but he is working at coping with his fears, and that he turns to God to help him do that, just as the author of Psalm 23 writes, "I shall fear no evil *for Thou art with me.*"

Eighty times God tells our ancestors not to be afraid. I want to focus on one of those times. When I verified the claim about that being the sentence occurring most frequently in the Bible, I shared that insight with my friend Rabbi Jack Riemer, and he responded by sharing with me an insight into one occurrence of that phrase that meant a lot to him.

It happened to Jacob late in his life. You may remember the story from the Bible. Jacob had twelve sons. He favored one of them, Joseph, over the others, and in their jealousy, the other brothers sold him as a slave to a passing caravan and told their father that he had been killed by a wild animal. Joseph ended up in Egypt, where he interpreted Pharaoh's dreams, advising him how to avoid a famine and make Egypt the only country in the area with enough food for its people and a surplus to sell to foreigners. Joseph's brothers came to buy food, and Joseph revealed his identity to them twenty years after they had sold him into slavery. He invited them and their by-now-elderly father to move to Egypt, where Joseph would provide for them.

The brothers then return home and tell Jacob that Joseph is alive, that he is an important government official in Egypt, and that he wants them to move there to live with him. Jacob immediately begins to make plans to relocate his family to Egypt.

It is at this point that God appears to Jacob. God hasn't spoken to him once in the past twenty years, which the Midrash explains by saying that the spirit of God does not abide with a person when he is angry or grieving. But God speaks to him now, and God says to Jacob, "*Al tira*, Don't be afraid." God makes three promises to Jacob: "I will go down to Egypt with you, I will bring you and your family back, and your son Joseph will close your eyes."

I want to focus on those three promises, because God understands even before Jacob does what Jacob is afraid of.

First, "Don't be afraid to go down to Egypt because I will be with you." Jacob is about to enter a new stage in his life. He doesn't know what is in store for him, but he does know two things: change is inevitable and change is scary. Change means leaving the familiar for the unknown. Once before, you may remember, God spoke to Jacob when he was leaving the familiar for the unknown. It happened when he was an adolescent leaving home because he had cheated his brother and deceived his father to gain the blessing that was meant for his brother. That time, God reassured him that, although he was leaving his parents' home and leaving the land of Canaan, he was not leaving God behind. God would be accessible to him at the house of Laban as God had been at his parents' home. Now once again, many years and many experiences later, Jacob is about to leave the land of Canaan and make his way to a new land. This time, he is not exchanging adolescence for adult responsibility, as he did the first time he left home, facing the uncertainty of marriage, of parenthood, of earning a living and establishing his identity. That was the first time God spoke to him. This time, he is exchanging the role of head of the household, being a mature adult responsible for his own well-being and that of those around him, for the role of an old man in an unfamiliar setting, sustained and supported by others. That scares him, and that is why God comes to him now and reassures him, "Don't be afraid."

Now do you see why I chose this passage to focus on? It's Yom Kippur, when we recite the prayer about "what is the New Year going to be like? A year of health and prosperity, or a year of illness and financial concern? A year of new people coming into our lives, or a year of people leaving us?" There are people who are facing the same kind of uncertainty that Jacob faced in the Bible. Maybe they are contemplating changing jobs, even changing careers. Maybe their children are grown and they are thinking of selling their home and moving into smaller quarters, and at some level it gives them the feeling that their world is shrinking. There are people who look at the horizon and see the end of their working life approaching, or perhaps they are wondering how much longer their current job will be viable. And they are asking themselves, as Jacob must have been asking himself: "Who will I be when I am no longer bringing home a paycheck? Who will I be when I'm no longer in charge of a household and a family?" There are people for whom the coming year will represent a new family arrangement—some of you adding, some of you sub-tracting—and you are understandably apprehensive about how that will work out.

God doesn't answer Jacob's concerns directly, but He does answer them when He says, "I will go down to Egypt with you." God is saying, "Yes, the future is unknown. The future is by definition always unknown. But you have to believe that, whatever the future holds, you will be up to the challenge. Look at what you've already done. You've worked your way through problems before. I was with you in hard times in Aram and in Canaan, and I'm not about to abandon you now."

God says to Jacob, "Don't think only about what you are leaving behind. Think of the new experiences awaiting you, and the opportunities for growth and for remaining vital that these new experiences will repre-sent, because facing and mastering new situations will keep you young and vital." God's second promise, "I will bring you and your offspring back," speaks to Jacob's second fear. If Jacob was afraid, on the one hand, that Egypt would not work out as a home for him and his family, that they would not fit in, at the same time he is afraid that it will work out all too well, that his children and grandchildren will feel too much at home in Egypt and forget that they are the descendants of Abraham, Isaac, and Jacob. And again you see why this is a passage that speaks to us today. We have been accepted in America, integrated into American life, more than our parents and grandparents could ever have imagined. My father spent the first twenty years of his life in Lithuania, but he never thought of himself as Lithuanian. He didn't speak Lithuanian; he spoke Hebrew and Yiddish. Even more so, the Jews of Germany, who spoke German, wrote important books in German, contributed to the cultural life of Germany, in fact virtually *were* the cultural life of Germany, were never permitted to forget that they were part of a separate community. But in this country in the past fifty years, we have been accepted. The bigots, the anti-Semites have been marginalized. If two generations ago, Jack Benny and Danny Kaye had to change their names to make it in show business, nobody asked that of Jerry Seinfeld or Barbra Streisand. We have been accepted and we are grateful for it. But at the same time, we share Jacob's fear. We worry that our children and grandchildren will become so assimilated—in the clothes they wear, in the music they listen to, in the pop stars they idolize—that they will forget that they are Jewish. God's promise is that they may wander, they may find an Egypt to travel to psychologically, but they will find their way back. If God's Covenant with Abraham is true, if the Revelation at Sinai is true, the truth will ultimately win out. People will come to recognize it. If the bond between parents and children is strong, if we don't overreact to an adolescent slamming the door to her room by slamming doors of our own, then that bond will exert a gravitational pull strong enough to keep offspring from wandering too far.

And it seems to me to be happening. Thirty years ago, bright young Jews were traveling to India and Nepal to study Buddhism. Today, non-Jewish Hollywood celebrities are studying Kabbalah (although as some of you have heard me say, the Kabbalah that Madonna is studying in Los Angeles is authentic Kabbalah to the same degree that she is an authentic Madonna). There are serious books being written, college courses being offered, adult classes proliferating, creative options for worship and study, to a degree that we have never seen before. Who could have foreseen a generation ago that Chabad houses would be as ubiquitous as Starbucks? In the spiritual world as in the culinary world, people are coming to realize that junk food may be tempting but is ultimately harmful, and are finding their way back to the real thing.

There is a Jewish legend about how Shma Yisrael became the quintessential declaration of Jewish faith. It bases itself on an incident at the very end of the book of Genesis, the very end of Jacob's life in Egypt. Jacob is dying. He calls Joseph to his bedside and asks Joseph to bring his children, Jacob's grandchildren, so that he can bless them. Jacob then goes on at great length praising his grandchildren, telling Joseph how much he loves them, as if they were his own children. Then, the Bible says, he looks at Joseph's children, Menasseh and Ephraim, and asks, "*Mi eleh*? Who are those kids?" And Joseph has to explain to him, "Those are the children with whom God has blessed me."

According to the Midrash, why doesn't Jacob recognize his own grandchildren, the ones he has just been talking about, saying how much he loves them? Not because his eyesight is failing, as happened to his father, Isaac. He doesn't recognize them because they look like Egyptian children. Born and raised in Egypt, their dress, their appearance is no different from that of the young people around them. And that bothers Jacob deeply. When he asks, "Who are those young people?" he is really asking, "I know what their names are, but who are they? Are they Jewish children? Are they part of our family, part of our people, with the same commitments and loyalties? Or have they become Egyptian children with Jewish parents?"

And Menasseh and Ephraim, sensing their grandfather's concern, answer him, "*Shma Yisrael*, Listen, Israel," (remember, Jacob's other name is Israel), "*Adonai Eloheinu*, the Lord is our God. We may look different, we may act different, but we still believe in the same God, the same Covenant, the same values, the same bloodstained and tearstained history that you do." And ever since then, Jewish parents have blessed their sons on the eve of the Sabbath, saying, "May you be like Ephraim and Menasseh, fully integrated into the society you live in and, at the same time, loyal and learned members of the Jewish people." As God is immortal, as the Torah is immortal, God's promise that the Jewish people will continue to be His representative on earth, that He will guide them to find their way back from whatever Egypt they have wandered to, is equally eternal.

God's third promise to Jacob is perhaps the most interesting and the most relevant of the three. "Joseph will close your eyes." Do you understand the reference? When a person dies, if he should die with his eyes open, the final act of kindness one can perform for him is to close his eyes, to bring down the final curtain on his life.

What is Jacob worried about as he prepares to relocate to Egypt? He hasn't spoken to Joseph for twenty years, since the day he disappeared and was presumed dead. I imagine Jacob thinking to himself, "How does he feel about me after all these years? Is he angry at me for neglecting him? Does he blame me for favoring him and making his brothers jealous? Has he made a new life for himself that has no room for me in it?"

I can imagine Jacob saying to himself, "There were so many times when I wasn't a very good father, when I made mistakes, when I had my priorities wrong. Will Joseph take this opportunity to get even with me?" And the greatest fear, the one he can't even put into words, is: *I don't want to die alone, with nobody caring for me.*

Over the years, members of the congregation have told me their stories: stories of estrangements, of family members not speaking to each other, of feuds going back so many years that nobody remembers how they started. There were the funerals where families would sit shiva in two or three different homes because the brothers and sisters didn't get along and they weren't going to let their Momma's death change that. There was the woman who told me that she wasn't going to say Kaddish for the father who had abused her physically and psychologically, and I tried to persuade her to say Kaddish, not to mourn the man who died but to grieve for the father she always wanted to have and never did, and now it was too late. There was even one funeral I officiated at where the surviving children couldn't agree on how the family name was pronounced. Sometimes the encounter with mortality forces people to open their eyes and realize what they are missing; sometimes it finds the fault line in a family and drives people further apart.

You came to me with your stories: the elderly parent who accepted the invitation to move in with her children, only to find herself left alone all day with the dog and the television set in a town with no public transportation; the elderly parent who lived with her children and grandchildren but couldn't get her daughter to accommodate her food limitations; and at the other end, the couples who invited a widowed parent to live with them with the best will in the world, only to find themselves with no privacy and an endlessly needy parent. And behind all the stories lies the desperate, unspoken fear: *I don't want to die alone.* Elderly parents are understandably frightened as they grow old and dependent: Will this be payback time for every argument, every restriction, every resentment held on to for decades or long buried but revived at this moment?

So Jacob is frightened as he prepares to move to Egypt to live with Joseph, and God has to reassure him. God has to say to him, "Your father, Isaac, wasn't a very good father. He favored your brother, Esau, over you. He never appreciated the things that made you special, that made you the rightful heir to the tradition of Abraham. He didn't know how to help you get what you wanted and needed in life. And you weren't a very good son. You lied to him, you deceived him. You sided with your mother against him. But in the end, you came back and were able to love him. You and Esau outgrew your conflicts, and when your father died, the two of you came together to bury him and mourn for him." Reconciliation is possible. Forgiveness is possible. It may not be easy but it can happen, and it is so much better than the alternative.

And then finally that moment comes. Jacob makes the long journey to Egypt. Joseph is there to welcome him. What were they thinking at that moment? "Was Joseph thinking, I can't remember what it was like to have a father, a loving father who cared for who I was and not just what I could do for him?" Was Jacob thinking, "How will Joseph handle this role reversal, my being dependent on him?"

Jacob arrives in Egypt and Joseph is there to greet him. They embrace, they kiss, they cry. And Jacob responds to Joseph's embrace by saying "*Amuta hapa'am*, Now I can die," which I take to mean: Now I'm not afraid of facing the end of my life, because I know I won't be facing it alone. The love that had lain dormant below the surface for all those years is recovered in one moment of mutual need and mutual forgiveness. Jacob settles into life in Egypt. Joseph presents him in court. He is proud of his father. And when Jacob dies, Joseph is there to close his eyes and tend to his burial.

It's Yom Kippur. It is the day when we spend the whole day in shul trying to plaster over the cracks in our lives, trying to put together the pieces of our lives so that we will start the New Year whole and not broken. And of all the things that frighten us, of all the dire things the New Year may have in store for us, from terrorism in this country to war in the Middle East, from loss of health to loss of jobs, I suspect that there is no prospect more frightening than the fear that we won't be able to tear down the walls that have somehow sprung up between us and other people in our lives and that, when problems come along, we'll have to face them alone.

But if the challenge is tearing down the walls that separate us, if the challenge is building bridges to reconnect us to people we really care about, that is one challenge we will not have to face alone. God promises us, as He promised Jacob, that He wants us to do it, that He understands how intimidating a prospect it is to make ourselves vulnerable to rejection as the inevitable risk of caring for someone, but He will be with us to give us the courage.

The last words ever spoken by a prophet in Israel, the last line of the last of the biblical prophets Malachi, reads: "*Hineh adnochi scholeach lacrem et Eliyah hanavi lifney bo hayom hagadol,* I am going to send you the prophet Elijah just before the dawning of the messianic era, *V'hesniv lev avotel banim v'lev banimel avotam,* and he will help bring about the one thing in the world that is lacking to make this world the messianic kingdom." He will connect the hearts of parents to their children and the hearts of children to their parents. He will teach us to love each other again, and then the world will be ready to be redeemed. God's promise at the outset of a New Year is the same promise He extended to Jacob many years ago, not that it will be a year free of problems, free of conflict. It will be a year with its share of problems—change and conflict and uncertainty—but we will be up to the challenge because whenever we set out to do the right thing, God will be at our side until all that is broken will be made whole again.

THE BLINDNESS OF ISAAC

When I was seventeen years old, I failed a test that I had been confident I would pass easily, and every day of my life since then, for more than sixty years, I have had to deal with the consequences of that failure. If that surprises you, if you would like to think that I was mature enough to get over that already, let me add one fact that may help you understand: the test I failed was the eye exam for a driver's license. Until that day, it had never occurred to me that I needed glasses. I thought the world was supposed to look fuzzy. But, since then, every morning when I wake up, one of the first things I have to do is reach for my glasses. As a result, I feel a sense of kinship with all the other people who have less-than-perfect vision.

Now, as you may remember, there is a story in the Torah about a man whose failing eyesight caused all sorts of complications in his family. The man was Isaac, who figures so prominently in our Rosh HaShanah readings from the Torah. We read, "When Isaac grew old, his eyes were dim and he could no longer see clearly." He sets out to designate his son Esau to inherit the leadership of the family and carry on the heritage of

Abraham, rather than Esau's twin brother, Jacob, who is their mother Rebecca's favorite.

Rebecca, who may be able to appreciate what was special about Abraham because he wasn't her father, sets out to disguise Jacob and fool Isaac into giving him the paternal blessing.

As I read the story, I began to suspect that Isaac's vision problem was more than simply deteriorating eyesight, the sort of thing that could have been corrected had eyeglasses or Lasik surgery been invented back then. It's not just that he couldn't read the letters on the eye chart; it was a kind of moral blindness. He looked at his two sons and all he saw were the things that were obvious on the surface—Esau's physical strength and manliness and Jacob's quiet, stay-at-home temperament—and he had no way of recognizing that it was Jacob who had the capacity for spiritual greatness that characterized Isaac's father, Abraham.

Sometimes, maybe even most of the time, people's most important qualities are not visible to the casual observer. I read a story some years ago about a young single woman on a blind date with a young pediatrician. Their mothers were friends who played cards together and had been trying for months to get the two young people to go out together. Finally the daughter agreed.

The evening did not start well. The couple went for dinner and the first thing that happened was that the pediatrician spilled soup on his tie. She tried to ask him about his work and he either grunted or answered in monosyllables. She sat there wondering how much longer she would have to put up with this before she could invent a headache and ask to be taken home, where she had a pint of Häagen-Dazs in the freezer.

Suddenly the doctor's beeper went off. He answered it and said to his date, "I'm terribly sorry. There's an emergency at the hospital and it involves something I'm the authority on. Would you mind stopping in with me? It shouldn't take more than a few minutes, and then I'll take you home." Would she mind? She'd much rather be in an emergency room full of crying children than trying to make conversation with this guy in a restaurant.

But at the hospital, something very interesting happened. Watching the doctor interact with a frightened, crying child, she saw qualities of gentleness and a sense of humor emerge that she would not have expected from him. To her astonishment, she found herself daydreaming about what kind of husband and father he might become. She remembers thinking to herself, "It's not a matter of settling for someone nobody else wants because I don't deserve better. It's a case of the experiences of my life opening my eyes to dimensions of people that my friends are blind to. And maybe the experiences of this man's life, the rejections and the loneliness, have opened his eyes to things about me that no one ever appreciated before." Her eyes had been opened and the world suddenly looked different to her.

When we look at the people around us, when we look at the people closest to us (and you know it's a law of nature that it's hard to see the people closest to you accurately), we need to train our eyes to see things that are not readily visible. My colleague Rabbi Harold Schulweis of Encino, California, once commented that today's Jewish parents have invented a new form of child abuse. It's called "being disappointed." All we see is that they're not getting straight As, they're not making the team, and we're not able to hide our disappointment from them. I can imagine a day when the United States will elect a Jewish president, and on the day of his inauguration, a reporter will ask his mother, "How do you feel on this momentous occasion? You must be very proud of him." And she will answer, "Actually, we hoped he would be a doctor."

But what about the qualities that don't translate into letters and numbers? I remember Dennis Prager, in this sanctuary many years ago, challenging the congregation—some of you may even remember it—by asking us, "How often have you praised your children for being smart, for getting good grades? And how often have you praised them for being kind?" Yet which of those attributes would Judaism put at the top of a good person's wish list?

Isaac got the easy part right. He saw the things that Esau did well. But he missed the more important part, the less obvious things that Jacob excelled at and Esau had no talent for, but those were the qualities that would go on to shape the Jewish future.

We read the Torah's account of how Jacob was able to pass himself off as his brother, Esau, and perhaps we wonder why Isaac could be so easily fooled. The boys were twins but they were far from identical. They looked, they sounded, they even smelled different. Why didn't Isaac catch on?

There is a beautiful midrash about why Isaac's vision was so bad and why he couldn't tell the difference between his deserving and his undeserving son. Think of the story we read every year on Rosh HaShanah, about how God told Abraham to offer his son Isaac as a sacrifice and then intervened at the last moment to tell him that he didn't have to. Picture that crucial moment: Isaac is lying on his back, bound on the altar, when the heavens open and God's angel appears over Abraham's shoulder with the message. At that moment, Isaac is looking directly into heaven, without the filter of clouds or even atmosphere. He sees into heaven with an undiluted intensity human eyesight is not designed for, and ever after that, he can no longer see normally. How does it affect him? Having seen the purity of heaven, he can no longer recognize falsehood. He can only see purity. He can only see the good in people. You can lie to him, you can fool him, and he won't recognize it. He's like the character created by Isaac Bashevis Singer, Gimpel the Fool.

Last February, I was invited to give a public lecture in Newtown, Connecticut, to try to help people come to terms with why God would let such a thing as the shooting death of all those little children happen. I spoke about my understanding of why bad things happen to innocent victims and what a proper response might be. And then, at the end, because it was Newtown, Connecticut, I added just a few words on the issue of gun control. I tried not to get too political or too controversial, so I told the audience, "My position on gun control has two elements. First, anyone who is mentally ill should not have access to an assault weapon. And second, anyone who believes that he needs an assault weapon to protect his family against an invasion of the United States by United Nations forces can be assumed to be mentally ill."

I was greeting people and signing books after the talk when one man took issue with what I had said. He challenged me, "Don't you think that if the Jews of Poland had had guns and known how to use them, more of them might have survived?" I wasn't expecting that question, so the only answer that came to my mind was the one I heard from Jon Stewart on *The Daily Show*: "If I recall, the French army had guns and knew how to use them, and how much good did it do them?"

It was only an hour or so later, when driving home, that I realized there was a better answer I could have given him. I could have said, "Yes, if the Jews of Eastern Europe had been more proficient in handling guns, if they had learned to hunt (even if they wouldn't have been able to eat anything they killed), they might have been able to better defend themselves. But then they would have been very different people from who they were, at home with violence, comfortable with the prospect of hurting another human being, people prepared to suspect the worst of their neighbors. So when Hitler and Stalin came along, they were vulnerable."

What do we lose when we lose the blindness of Isaac, when the reality of life compels us to be skeptical of the salesman, to read the small print in the ads carefully, when we learn to be suspicious of strangers? Supreme Court Justice Sonia Sotomayor tells in her autobiography why she left her first job after law school, as an assistant district attorney in New York City, even though she enjoyed it, learned a lot, and did a lot of good. She writes, "All around me, I saw personalities distorted by cynicism and despair. Trained in suspicion, skilled at cross-examination, you are always looking for the worst in people, and if you look hard enough, you will find it." She is warning us of the price we pay when we can no longer look at the world through the trusting eyes of a child. If we don't want the dishonesty of bad people to corrode the health of our souls, we need to find some place of refuge, be it our homes, our synagogue, a volunteer or civic group, where we can be with people who are trying to do good and are not out to take advantage of us, places like the world that Isaac glimpsed when the heavens opened for him.

Isaac's blindness kept him from seeing the less obvious gifts of his son

Jacob. The father's innocence made it hard for him to know when he was being lied to. Yet there is another form of moral blindness that is a lot more harmful. It's the difficulty some people have in seeing that there is something wrong with what they are doing. How could somebody not understand that setting off a bomb in a crowd, killing and maiming innocent people, was wrong, irrespective of what you think of American foreign policy? How could Bernard Madoff not have realized that stealing from people who trusted him was wrong, and not something he was entitled to do because he was smarter than everybody else? What kind of person steals from Elie Wiesel in order to buy himself a mansion in Palm Beach? What kind of person defrauds and impoverishes lifelong friends, cheats people who use their investment income to sustain charities, and doesn't see anything wrong with it? That must be an extreme case of moral blindness.

When one of the most uplifting sports stories of recent years turned out to be based on lies and fraud, when Lance Armstrong finally admitted that all of his cycling wins were the result of cheating and all the lawsuits threatening people who questioned him were attempts to intimidate investigations, perhaps the most insightful comment anyone made about him was the comment made by one reporter who characterized his confession as "guilt without shame." Armstrong admitted that he had broken the rules, but so what? He was using his cleverness to get things he wasn't entitled to; what's so terrible about that?

"Guilt without shame." But I would submit that shame, the capacity to feel uncomfortable when you realize you've done something wrong, is the defining characteristic of a human being. There is something deficient about us as human beings if we can't feel it. That's why the word "rationalize" exists in the English language, so that we can persuade ourselves that something we know is wrong isn't really that bad.

The capacity to feel shame, the perception that some things are just wrong—not just against the law, not just a violation of the rules, but wrong—is what makes us different from animals and defines us as human. That, I will insist, is the real meaning of the Garden of Eden story in the Torah. It's not about Original Sin. Go back and read chapter 3 of Genesis and count how often the word "sin" occurs there. You know how many times? Zero. God never calls what Eve and Adam do a sin, let alone a misdeed their descendants will inherit the guilt for.

Remember the name of the fruit they ate? It wasn't simply "the fruit you're not supposed to eat." It was "the fruit of the knowledge of Good and Evil." By eating it, they acquired something that no other creature in the world had, the awareness that some things are right and some are wrong. Not just harmful, not just something you can be punished for, but morally wrong. No animal can understand that concept; no small child can understand it. And as we repeatedly discover, even some teenagers and even some adults don't get that message. Bernard Madoff and Lance Armstrong seem not to have understood that. Adolf Hitler and the millions of Germans who followed him seem not to have understood that. But that is the one quality that defines someone as a human being. As I read that third chapter of Genesis, Eve is not the villain of the piece. She is the heroine. She is the first human being in history, the first of God's creatures to bravely step across the line that separates us from other animals and enter the landscape of moral responsibility.

If you were paying close attention to the Torah readings on Rosh HaShanah, you noticed that they were all about people learning to see the world differently. Abraham welcomes three strangers into his tent and perceives that they are messengers from God, and for the rest of his life, he will see the image of God in everyone he meets, and he will teach his descendants to do the same. Hagar, Abraham's handmaid, finds herself cast out and abandoned, rejected by everyone. She is at the point of despair, about to die of thirst in the desert, when we read "her eyes were opened and she saw a well of life-giving water." The well had been there all along, but in her despair, she never noticed it. For the rest of her life, I would like to think that she would never give up on the world. She would never stop hoping that the world will yet turn out to be a more livable place than it might seem at the moment. And Isaac, bound on the altar and facing death, suddenly saw the heavens open and saw things no mortal had ever seen, and he never got over that moment. For the rest of his life, no matter what happened to him, he would look at other people and like them, without envy and without suspicion.

And we who have shared moments of prayer and Torah study, if we can let a synagogue service do for us what the events of their lives did for Abraham, for Hagar, for Isaac; if we can let it open our eyes so that we can see clearly; if we can learn to see the not-so-obvious gifts hidden in the souls of our partners, our children, our neighbors; if we can see the wrongness of things we might otherwise be tempted by, then this morning may indeed be the first day of a good New Year.

PEOPLE WHO NEED PEOPLE

One week last winter, at a time when millions of Americans were reading books about vampires and zombies, I was reading a book about the Frankenstein monster. Why was I reading about the Frankenstein monster? My grandson had been assigned the book for his tenth-grade English class and told me how much he enjoyed it, and I wanted to share the experience with him.

The book was written in 1818 by Mary Shelley, the wife of the poet Percy Bysshe Shelley. She wrote it in the early days of the Industrial Revolution to say something about the danger of humans arrogating to themselves powers that had previously belonged exclusively to God. As many of you probably know, it's the story of a brilliant but perverse scientist who had learned how to bring inanimate matter to life. He fashions a human figure out of spare parts and animates it, like God creating Adam in the opening pages of the Bible. The creature is large, powerful, and very strange-looking (all those mismatched body parts). He goes on to take revenge on his creator for miscreating him by killing everyone whom Dr. Frankenstein loves. But beyond the message about the danger of humans trying to play God, the book taught me an important lesson about what it means to be human, and although I don't think Mary Shelley had this in mind when she wrote the book two hundred years ago, it helped me understand why, when Jews come to shul on Shabbat, they insist on sitting in the back rows. More about that later.

There is an important incident about a third of the way through the book that for me is the key to what the book is all about. The creature has been assembled and brought to life, and sent out into the world. Somehow he has learned to speak English and French. Wandering through the woods somewhere in Switzerland, he spies this little cottage occupied by a blind old man and his daughter and son-in-law. The creature feels kindly toward them, so every night he gathers food and firewood and leaves it at their doorstep. Every morning they find his gifts waiting for them. Not knowing where they came from, they offer a blessing of gratitude to whatever mysterious force put them there.

This goes on for about two weeks. The creature hears their expressions of gratitude and feels the stirrings of love in his heart. These people can be his friends. So one day, when the young couple are out, he knocks on the door and is invited in by the blind old man. He tells the man that he is the one who has been leaving all these gifts every night, and the old man blesses him for it. The two of them have a pleasant chat until the daughter and son-in-law return. They see this strange-looking creature close to their father and they assume he is trying to hurt him. They attack the creature with sticks, stones, furniture until he runs out of the house. Although he could easily hurt them, he chooses not to, and runs away in despair. He thought they would be his friends, and he is deeply hurt that they rejected him. It's at that point that he realizes no one will ever accept him and love him because of who he is, and he decides to become a monster and take his revenge on his creator for making him as he is.

Now, there are a lot of ways of interpreting that incident. It can be about the way we treat people who look different. But to me, it says something about what it means to be a human being. A human being is shaped by sharing his or her life with other human beings. No matter how pure your intentions, you can't be authentically human all by yourself. People need people to be people.

Many years ago, I took a college course in anthropology, from which I remember only one sentence: one chimpanzee cannot be a chimpanzee. He needs a community of chimps before his essential nature can emerge. And in much the same way, one human being isolated from others cannot really be a human being, cannot be what a human being is meant to be. We need the companionship of others to let our humanity emerge.

There is a passage in the Talmud in which one of the Sages, Rabbi Joshua ben Levi, suggests that when you run into a friend whom you haven't seen for a year, you should recite a blessing, "*Baruch m'chayeh ha-metim*, Praise God who has brought the dead to life." That's usually understood, and for years I understood it, to mean that if a person, someone you feel close to, hasn't been a part of your life for an entire year, it's as if that person ceased to exist; but now that he's restored to you, now that he's come back into your life, it's as if he has come back to life altogether. But I wonder if maybe we can understand it differently. Maybe from Rabbi Joshua's perspective, the one who had been brought back to life is not the friend whom you haven't seen for a while. Maybe it's you. You have been less fully alive, you have been living your life less fully, without the gift of human companionship this friend represents.

Fifty-five years ago, Erich Fromm wrote that our sanity depends on being connected to other people. Think about all the stories you've read about the man who suddenly explodes in an outburst of rage, killing somebody, setting fires, destroying something. Reporters talk to the neighbors and what do they always say? "He seemed like such a nice guy, quiet, a bit of a loner, kept to himself, never seemed to have any friends or visitors." But maybe having no friends or visitors sets a person up for that kind of outburst. Human beings need to share their lives with other human beings to keep themselves human.

Once upon a time, in fact for most of human history, we did that pretty well. For many of us when we were young, the people we interacted with were neighbors: we knew their names—the grocer, the pharmacist, the crossing guard. But then, as society became more complex, it became less personal. Now the people we deal with—clerks, service providers, and salespeople—are strangers. In one generation, we've gone from *Cheers*, where everybody knew your name, to Starbucks, where no matter how often you go in there, you get the feeling they've never seen you before. We used to live in neighborhoods, but last summer an article in *Parade* magazine described how the kinds of houses people are building these days distance them from their neighbors so that people living near each other don't know each other except to nod hello. There are no neighborhoods anymore.

Or even worse, we don't deal with people at all. We deal with machines. We're asked to pump our own gas, to bag our own groceries, to press "one" for a list of options and then punch in our credit card number. I sometimes wonder if the pervasive crankiness and irritability that seems to afflict so many Americans is the result of our being deprived of an essential vitamin that we need for our well-being, the vitamin of genuine human contact. Are we in danger of suffering the fate of Dr. Frankenstein's creature, becoming less human than we aspire to be because our interactions with other people are so meager?

Some years ago, researchers set out to measure the level of happiness in different cultures. They studied societies all over the world to see where the most people reported the highest level of happiness in their lives. They found out some interesting things. Widespread poverty left people unhappy, but widespread wealth didn't necessarily make them happier. The happiest societies were ones where people could trust their neighbors, and the least happy ones were places where ethnic and tribal rivalries meant you couldn't count on your neighbors not to hurt or cheat you. Human beings need to share their lives with other human beings to know what it means to be human.

A couple of years ago, in a casual conversation, a friend told me about something that had happened to her when she was younger. She was at a crossroads in her life. She had to make a decision and couldn't figure out what to do. She had been studying Buddhism, so she went to the Zen master she had been studying with and shared her dilemma, and he told her a Zen story that helped her decide. I told her, "That's a great story. I'm working on a book about resources that help people cope with their fears, and that would fit perfectly into my last chapter. Is it OK with you if I used it? I'd change enough of the details so nobody would know it was you." She said, "I'd rather you didn't. It's a very personal story, and if I ever get around to writing something I'm thinking about, I might want to use it." I said, "OK, fine, I won't use it."

Three days later, I got a letter from her lawyer, enjoining me from ever using the story and asking me to sign an agreement that, if I did use it, I would concede that I had been guilty of plagiarism. I signed it, and then I called her and said, "What's going on? I thought we were friends. I told you I wouldn't use it. I gave you my word. Did you really have to get a lawyer involved?" She said, "You just can't trust people these days, and if you did print it, it would be too late to do anything." Is that what we've come to these days? And is that why there is so much negativity, so much hostility in the air?

If that is the problem, what is the answer? Let me suggest that the cure can be found in this room. That's what we do here: we take individuals and turn them into a community. Just about a hundred years ago, a pioneering French sociologist named Émile Durkheim, grandson of the former chief rabbi of Paris, set out for a remote South Sea island to study the most primitive forms of religion he could find, to try to learn what religion looked like before it got involved with sacred books and creeds and professional clergy. Durkheim discovered that, at its most basic, the first and most essential task of religion was not to connect people to God, but to connect them with one another so that together they could invoke the feeling of being in the presence of God. The purpose of religion, Durkheim suggested, is to make sure that when you need not to be alone, you won't have to be alone, and to help you find God in the company of other seekers. When you've suffered a loss, when you've been rejected, or even when you have something to celebrate, a birth or a bar mitzvah, you want to share that moment with other people, people who know you and care about you and aren't trying to sell you anything. In the same year that Freud wrote that grieving for a loss is the most private and individual thing a person will ever do, that no one else can possibly understand what you are feeling, Durkheim wrote that grieving really works only when it is a social process.

Freud would tell us that your loss is a very private matter. What happens when you lose someone you love? You feel singled out by adverse fate. You have the sense that the world is full of happy, intact families and only you are grieving. But then you come to temple, to the minyan, and you enter a very different world, a world where many of the people around you are bereaved and the others are there because when they were in mourning, people were there for them and they want to do that for you. Suddenly your world is less empty, less lonely. Community has started to fill the vacuum.

Why were the churches and synagogues filled to capacity on the weekend after 9/11? Not because we believed that our prayers could make that terrible event unhappen. We came because at some level, we needed to be reassured that God had not abandoned us, and we instinctively knew that we had a better chance of hearing that message of hope and reassurance if we didn't have to look for it alone.

If our society is sick today because people are starved for human connection, and if religion is all about connecting people with each one another no ulterior motive except to help them fulfill their humanity, if it and it alone possesses the magic that would have kept Dr. Frankenstein's creature from becoming a monster and could have helped him become human, then maybe we need religion, maybe we need religious community, in a way we never realized we did. If we're putting an unfair and unbearable strain on our families by asking them to do more for us than they are capable of doing (it's hard enough just being a family without having to be someone's community as well), and if our work has become increasingly kidnapped by technology so that it affords us too little human companionship, then maybe we need to find moments of human interaction outside the home and beyond the workplace. If we need to share our lives with other people to know what it means to be human, and if being Jewish is the Jewish way of being human, then we can't really be Jewish all by ourselves. Being Jewish can't be a private matter, a question of what you believe about God and the Torah. Being Jewish is what you share with other Jews.

I wonder how many of you had the same reaction to Chelsea Clinton's wedding that I did. Part of me got a kick out of how Jewish the ceremony was. It used to be that, when people of different faiths married, the service was a Christian ceremony with a Reform rabbi trundled in at the end to mumble a benediction. At the Clinton-Mezvinsky wedding, it was virtually a Jewish service, with a *ketubah*, a chuppah, the groom wearing a yarmulke, and breaking a glass, and a token presence of a Methodist minister. It said something about how fully Judaism has been integrated into the American scene. That was part of me. The other part of me felt saddened that it reinforced the idea that being Jewish is a private matter; I have my identity and you have yours. It's not. Judaism is not something that happens in an individual heart and soul. It's something that happens in a family, a congregation, a community.

And that brings me to the other insight I gained from reading *Frankenstein*, why Jews who come to shul with some regularity like to sit in back. It's not so that they can get to the Kiddush faster, and it's not a matter of keeping their distance from the rabbi and cantor. The reason is very simple. When you sit in the front rows, you see a performance. You see the cantor davening, the rabbi speaking, the bar mitzvah boy chanting his haftarah. But when you sit in back, you see a congregation.

You realize you are more than a spectator, that you are called on to participate, to be an invoker of the presence of God, not just a consumer of it.

There is such a thing as the holiness of community, moments when we join with other people for the sublime experience of transcending our isolation, our individuality, and becoming part of something greater than ourselves. That's why prayers of *kedusha*, prayers that respond to the presence of holiness—the Mourner's Kaddish, the reading of the Torah—require a minyan. They have to be said in public. And that's why at Shabbat service, the Kiddush, the socializing that follows the service, is as much a part of the Shabbat worship experience as the prayers themselves. Even the word "Kiddush" implies something made holy.

Realize if you will that we are social creatures. We are affected by the presence of those around us. That's why a funny movie or a scary movie is never as funny or as scary when you watch it at home as when you see it in a crowded theater. That's why you can see the ball game better at home on television, with close-ups and instant replay, but you experience the game better at the ballpark when one moment can cause thirty thousand people to stand up and cheer as one. And that is why, when we find it hard to sense God's presence in our daily lives, we can, if we're lucky, find it in the songs and in the silences of a congregational service.

We're not here this morning to tell God things He would otherwise not know, nor is it because God takes attendance and factors it into our grade for the coming year. We're here because there is a big blank page on our personal calendar marked 5771 by the Hebrew reckoning, and we're nervous about what is going to be written on that page. We sense that there is something missing in our lives, and we come to shul hoping to get a clue as to what it is and where we can find it.

Let me suggest that what we may be missing is the vitamin of human connection, of soul-to-soul contact rather than calculated transaction. We need it to be fully human and we don't get enough of it. If you don't find it at work, if you love your computer but you realize that it can't love you back, if it's asking too much of your family to provide all the friendship and all the emotional sustenance you need, please know that we are here every day and every week of the year for precisely that purpose, to do what we have been doing today, to nourish our humanity, to make us more human than we have ever been before. And if that happens, if we invite it into our lives and let it happen, then we will indeed have a *Shanah Tovah*, a Good Year for us all.

INVISIBLE PEOPLE

"It is determined on Rosh HaShanah and confirmed on Yom Kippur, who shall live and who shall die, who shall prosper and who shall suffer, who by weapon and who by wild beast..." They are the most familiar, and the most intimidating, words of a long Rosh HaShanah service. And then at the end, we conclude with a few hopeful words, "but repentance, prayer, and charity can avert the severity of the decree." In other words, the bad things may still happen, but if you are the right kind of person, they will hurt less. The severity will be less. How does that work? How do we make the painful things in life less painful? Let's begin by taking a look at some of the things that hurt us.

On Rosh HaShanah, we read of how Abraham's wife Sarah was concerned about the influence Ishmael, Abraham's son with the servant woman Hagar, might have on her son Isaac. So she persuaded Abraham to banish Ishmael and his mother.

The story is an echo of an earlier incident when Sarah is frustrated by her inability to conceive and bear a child, so she suggests to Abraham that they use the maidservant as a surrogate, that Abraham impregnate her and they adopt any child she bears him. But when Hagar does become pregnant, she starts acting superior to her master's wife because she has been able to do something the lady of the house couldn't do. Sarah can't handle this, so she mistreats the pregnant Hagar until she runs away. She flees into the wilderness, where God appears to her and tells her, "Don't be afraid. Everything will work out. Go back and bear your child. Call him Ishmael, meaning 'God has heard me.'" And then God goes on to say, "He will grow up to be a wild man, quarreling and fighting with everyone around him."

That's the part that interests me. How does God know that? How can God know in advance how Ishmael's life will turn out? Are these things really ordained in advance? I can think of two answers. One is that He's God, He knows everything. The other is that anyone looking at Ishmael's situation could have predicted that he would grow up angry at the world and have a short fuse. Look at his life. His mother is too overwhelmed by her own problems to be much of a parent to him. Did you notice what happens in this biblical story? Hagar and Ishmael are stuck in the desert. They've run out of food and water. The boy is thirsty; he cries for water. What does Hagar do? She says, "I'm sorry; I can't take this anymore." She puts him down and walks away.

Abraham, Ishmael's father, has his own family to take care of, and Abraham's wife is jealous of any attention her husband pays that other woman and her son. You don't have to be able to see into the future to be able to predict what Ishmael will be like when he grows up.

I recently ran across this quotation from the philosopher William James: "No more fiendish punishment can be devised than that one should be turned loose in society and remain unnoticed by everyone." That was Ishmael's fate. Nobody in his life cared about him. It's as if he was invisible. William James was right; that is about the most painful experience anyone can undergo.

What do invisible people do with their pain? There are two things you can do with pain. You can turn it inward on yourself and develop self-destructive behavior. Or you can turn it outward, so that the accumulated rage inside you explodes in an outburst of anger and violence. It's a pattern we may recognize from our own children: if you don't recognize them for being good, they will find a way to make you recognize them for being bad. Anything is better than being Invisible.

Does the name Columbine ring a bell, the Colorado high school where two unhappy loners with access to guns went on an orgy of killing classmates and teachers? Or Virginia Tech? Or all the other incidents in high schools and colleges across the country, all of them the same story: A young man (girls are more likely to hurt others with gossip than with guns) so resentful of the attention paid to athletes, prom queens, and straight-A students, sets out to do something that will meet two needs simultaneously. It will hurt those who ignored him, and it will get his name and picture on the news. Sometimes the person even leaves notes for friends and family: "By this time tomorrow, I'll be famous. Everybody will know who I am." In other words, he will no longer be an invisible person. And so many lives are hurt in the process.

Where else do we treat people as if they were invisible, as if they weren't there? I got a call one day last fall from a friend of mine in Minneapolis who said, "I see you're scheduled to come to town next month to promote your new book. Could you do me a tremendous favor and come a day early, and be the featured speaker at an event I'm planning? It's a dinner for people with eating disorders." I told her, "Terri, what a marvelous idea, a dinner for people with eating disorders! Maybe after dinner we can go out for drinks with the local Alcoholics Anonymous chapter." She explained to me that we would not be serving dinner to anorexics. It was to raise funds for a center to treat people with eating disorders. It seems that a prominent member of the community had a daughter who stopped eating to the point that it threatened her life. He was fortunate to find the right doctor who helped her, and in gratitude he wanted to establish a clinic where that doctor could help other people with the same problem.

The doctor was there that evening. I met him and he spoke just before I did. He told of the first time he met this young woman. He asked her, "Are you not eating so that you'll be more attractive?" She said, "No, I'm not eating in the hope that if I lose enough weight, I'll disappear and then I won't have to put up with those looks I get from everybody, looks of rejection, of revulsion because they don't like my appearance."

I had a colleague—he's deceased now—a much-loved rabbi named Yaacov Rosenberg. He was a large man, heavy-set; he probably weighed in excess of 250 pounds. He served a congregation in Philadelphia for many years, worked at the Seminary for a while, and when he retired, he moved to Israel. He told us the story once that he was in a post office in Jerusalem, waiting on line to mail a package, when a young woman walked in and breezed past him to the counter to be waited on. He politely tapped her on the shoulder and said, "Pardon me, miss, I believe I was here before you." She answered, "Oh, I'm sorry, sir, I didn't notice you." To which Rabbi Rosenberg, all 250 pounds of him, responded, "Miss, that's the most flattering thing anyone's said to me in years."

He was able to make a joke of it, but in fact we make a point of not noticing people who don't fit our arbitrary definition of what is attractive, and most of them don't find it funny. And the craziest part of it is that our standards of what it means to be attractive are constantly changing.

Last year, I read the memoir of the grandson of the man who invented Sweet'n Lo, the artificial sweetener. It was a fascinating book at many levels, and one of the things I learned from it is that saccharin, the first artificial sweetener, was approved for human consumption in 1912, the last year of the presidency of William Howard Taft. Woodrow Wilson would defeat him for re-election later that year. Why is that significant? Taft, one hundred years ago, was the last overweight man to be elected president of the United States. It may just be a coincidence, but it would almost seem that the invention of artificial sweeteners redefined what it meant to be good-looking. Do you remember what the most admired people looked like in the Gilded Age, just over a century ago, the Jay Goulds and J. P. Morgans and Lillian Russells? They were large, full-formed people, whose appearance testified to their ability to buy all the rich food they wanted. Back then, it was a source of shame for a man to be tanned and muscular; it meant he had to do physical labor outdoors. Standards of attractiveness change; the only thing that remains constant is our readiness to ignore people who don't meet those standards, to relegate them to the category of invisible people.

And then there is one other category of people whom we train ourselves not to notice, people whose shared humanity we have trouble recognizing. I was changing planes in Charlotte, North Carolina, one day and in the boarding area where we were waiting to get on our plane, there was a mother and a young child. You could tell that the boy had something wrong with him developmentally just by the way he walked and laughed. But he and his mother were having a wonderful time that afternoon. They were laughing, playing games, and chasing each other around the area. I remember thinking to myself, "I hope everybody is watching those two. I hope everybody is watching them and learning the lesson of how much you can enjoy a child who is less than perfect, how much you can enjoy a child who is seriously flawed, how easy it is to make them laugh and for them to make you laugh." But as I looked around, I realized that nobody was watching them. They all made a point of averting their eyes, perhaps because it reminded them of their own vulnerability and that of their own families, all the things that can go wrong with a person, how easily a person can fall victim to a genetic or physical flaw till they can no longer do what normal people do. They didn't want to see that, so they turned that mother and child and the elderly couple sitting near them into invisible people.

As William James understood a century ago, we generate so much pain in our world when we render so many people invisible. Sometimes we hurt the people we make a point of not noticing, and sometimes their pain and anger overflow and hurt people around them. What if anything do the High Holy Day prayers have to tell us about that? How can we reduce the severity of the anguish for all those people whose lives have been embittered by neglect or by genetic misfortune?

First, we can ease the pain of invisible people simply by noticing them. Remember, it is a mitzvah in Judaism to see all human beings as children of God, fashioned in the image of God. It is an offense against God, it is a desecration of God's image, to show disrespect or disregard for any human being. I never cease to marvel at the number of people who, if they drop a prayer book or a Humash, pick it up and kiss it to make up for having treated a sacred object with disrespect, but it never occurs to them to have to atone for treating one of God's human children with disrespect. If God is invisible, if God has no shape or form, might He not have a certain fondness for those of His creatures who are treated as if they were invisible here on earth? And if we yearn to see God and every human being as an image of God, how dare we violate that image by scorning any human being?

Second, we can help to heal the anguish of a fractured world by bringing ourselves to care more deeply about the Jewish people. Now, I know that sounds counterintuitive: How do you reduce the invisibility problem by caring more about Jews than about non-Jews? Leonard Fein explained it some years ago when he wrote about the brotherhood of men. Six billion brothers seemed too much for him to handle, so he started to think of it as a brotherhood of all Jews – and a cousinhood of all men instead.

What Fein was saying is that it's hard to train yourself to care about strangers, people you've never met and may have little in common with, people you might not even like if you were to get to know them. So practice caring on Jews you've never met and might not like if you did. Teach yourself to care about them. Share the dreams and feel the pain of Jews all over the world. Feel the pain of victims of terror in Israel. Feel the vulnerability of French and British Jews caught between the anti-Semitic rage of Muslim immigrants and the genteel condescension of the locals who never saw them as real Frenchmen or Britons to begin with. Empathize with the confusion of Russian Jews who were told in their native country, "you're not real Russians; you're Jews" and then when they move to Israel or the United States, are told "you're not real Jews; you're Russians." Then, when you've learned to do that, extend that habit of caring to the rest of the human race, to everyone who hurts, to everyone who suffers in silence.

Do you know the difference between shame and guilt? We tend to use the words interchangeably, as synonyms for the techniques our parents used to control us. But they are really different things in some important ways.

Psychologists will tell you that guilt is an auditory experience, a private phenomenon, a voice inside your head telling you that you did wrong. Shame is a visual experience, the sense of being looked at by others, judged, and found wanting.

Guilt is easier to cure. If the voice inside your head is nagging you about something you've done, do something good to make you feel better about yourself. Give charity, volunteer to help the needy, and the voice will stop.

Shame is more complicated, and it's really shame we're talking about when we speak of invisible people. You can't get rid of shame by yourself the way you can get out from under guilt by yourself. You need a supportive community. That is why twelve-step programs work. I've lost count of how many people I've met in the course of my travels who have told me privately that the most authentically religious experience they ever have comes not on Sunday mornings in the church sanctuary but on Tuesday evenings in the church basement when they go to their twelve-step group meeting. As one man put it, "I go to church, I hear judgment. I go to my therapist, I get explanations. I go to my twelve-step program, I feel acceptance." Acceptance is precisely what washes away shame, and acceptance is what invisible people crave so desperately.

When we come to that moment in the service when we say, "It is determined on Rosh HaShanah and confirmed on Yom Kippur...," what goes through your mind? Are you thinking, "What does the year hold in store for me and for my family?" Does it ever occur to you to say to yourself, "There are four hundred fellow congregants around me reciting the same words and a lot of them are worried about the same things I am. They're also afraid of what the coming year might hold in store for them. Are there any little things I can do to ease their fears, and maybe they would reciprocate and make me feel more hopeful about my own concerns?" That's why we have a congregational service on Rosh HaShanah instead of sending every family a Mahzor and telling them to read it at home.

Maybe the implication of that last line of the prayer—about how prayer, charity and a change of values diminish the severity of the decree—maybe it's trying to tell us on Rosh HaShanah that we should outgrow the self-centeredness that leads us to think that everything is about us. Maybe it wants us to think of ways in which we can make life more bearable for some of those other people, things we can do that will remove from them the cloak of invisibility, things that will erase their sense of shame and ease their fears. There are some things in life you just can't do for yourself, and getting rid of shame, the sense of being rejected by people around you, is one of them.

The high school student who goes out of his or her way to do something nice for a classmate who is not part of the "in" group, and does it without condescension or pity but simply as the reaching out of one vulnerable human soul to another, reduces the severity of the decree that other youngster is living with, the curse of wondering why God hasn't blessed him or her with the gifts He's given others. And the adult who reaches out to the marginal person, again not as a gesture of pity but as a mitzvah, a way of recognizing the presence of God in another human being, does the same blessed thing. You know what it's like at the daily minyan. When that door opens and the tenth person walks in, it doesn't matter who that person is, how knowledgeable or how personable. We all recognize that now there is more holiness in the chapel than there was a moment ago.

There is a short story by the Russian writer Turgenev about the man who is approached by a beggar, a particularly unpleasant-looking beggar, asking for a handout. He says to the beggar, "I'm sorry, my brother, I don't have my wallet with me." And the beggar says to him, "That's all right. You've given me something more valuable than money. You're the first person in years who has called me Brother."

The person who goes out of his way to help an elderly man or woman, again without pity and without impatience, eases his or her fear of growing old in a world that too often has little regard for older people, a world that prefers to see them as Invisible. And even if no one reciprocates and does that for you, and even if you don't particularly need having it done for you in return, doesn't it mean something that you have made this world a kinder place, a world in which even the decrees of misfortune have been attenuated?

I remember reading a short story some years ago called "Charity." It told of an observant Jewish family: a father, a mother, and a young son. The mother is hospitalized with cancer and her husband and child go to visit her. Leaving the hospital, they see a beggar on the street. The father gives the beggar a five-dollar bill. The boy says, "Now I know that Momma will get better, because at school the Rabbi taught us '*tzedaka tatzil mimavet*, giving charity saves people from death.'" The father answers him, "I believe it does save people, but maybe not Momma." The boy asks, "Then who does it save?" The father looks back at the beggar and says, "Him."

One commentator on the story notes that the last word of the story, "Him," is a one-word sentence, so the *H* is capitalized. It can refer to the beggar or it can refer to God, or it can refer to the beggar as an image of God, an incarnation of God. That is the power we have with our little deeds of thoughtfulness, the power if not to make other people's problems go away, then at least to diminish their severity and make them more bearable. We have the power to rescue souls from the Hell that William James spoke of, the Hell of going through life believing that no one sees you, no one cares about you, and in the process, we rescue God from being Invisible in this world, so that no one will have to doubt His existence when life is so harsh, and we make God more of a real presence in our world. Can there be a greater mitzvah than that?

GOOD ENOUGH FOR GOD

Yom Kippur is like no other day in the Jewish calendar, and to the best of my knowledge it has no counterpart in any other religion, with its twenty-four-hour abstention from eating and other physical concerns, with its wide-ranging moods, from guilt to radical self-acceptance, from the very private moments of being asked to examine our consciences to the collective reenactment of the expiation service as it was performed in ancient Jerusalem in days when the Temple stood. But if we were asked where the emotional center of the twenty-four hours of Yom Kippur is, I suspect most of us would fasten on the Yizkor service of memorial. On a day when the physical reality is of how many seats are filled, the emotional reality of Yizkor will always center on seats that were once filled but today stand empty, people who were part of our lives—parents, siblings, husbands, wives, children, friends—and are no longer physically here with us. Whatever else the Mahzor may be about, for most of us, I suspect, it will always lock in on memories of love and loss.

We all bring our memories of love and loss with us to synagogue on Yom Kippur, but there are families for whom Yizkor will be especially, perhaps even unbearably painful. There is a family in Newton who will be trying to come to terms with the death by suicide last February of their seventeen-year-old son.

He was one of three bright, promising Newton teenagers who took their own lives this past spring, young people from loving homes who seemed to have so much to live for. I didn't know any one of the three or their families, and I hesitate to diagnose someone I never met. How can you understand what would drive a young person with so much to live for to deliberately end his or her own life? But knowing what I do know of the stresses of being seventeen or eighteen years old in an affluent, status-conscious suburb, it's hard not to suspect that all three of them suffered from the same disease, and the name of that disease is: the fear of not being good enough. I know something of the anxiety, born of worry, that affects many young people of that age; whether it's the fear of not getting into the kind of college your parents expect you to or a bad midyear report card or a failed romantic relationship, the bottom line will inevitably be "What if I'm just not good enough? What kind of life can I have to look forward to?"

High schools can be cruel places when it comes to separating young people into winners and losers. I had a terrible time in high school. It was my introduction to all the ways in which some people are taken more seriously than others, and I was one of the others. I received weekly, if not daily, reminders that I was not part of the in crowd. Then, thirty five years after we graduated, I got a letter from a committee of my former high school classmates, inviting me to be the main speaker at our thirty-fifth reunion. This was right after *When Bad Things Happen to Good People* had been on the *New York Times* best-seller list for two years. I wrote back and politely declined, telling them I was sorry but it didn't fit into my schedule. Yet what I felt like writing was "Where were you when I needed you, when I was a shy, awkward fifteen-year-old and a kind word of recognition from one of you would have meant so much to me?"

But high school is only one example of all the ways in which some people are taken more seriously than others. There is the whole world of internet matchmaking. Can you imagine—I suspect many of you can—the humiliation of having someone meet you for thirty seconds and giving you the message "You're not worth my time"? There is the world of work, whether it's sales or management, where I sometimes think people work overtime to invent ways of rejecting other people. Is this really the kind of world we want our children to grow up into? No wonder some gifted, sensitive teenagers, even if they don't do something as drastic as those Newton teenagers did, find ways of telling us that this is not a game they are interested in playing.

Suburban parents are caught in a trap. I really believe that a very small part of it is about bragging rights when it comes to college acceptance, like that mythical bumper sticker that reads "My son is a student at Harvard" and then in small print "Also accepted at Yale, Cornell, and Johns Hopkins." I would like to think that very few parents are that self-centered, thinking their children's successes and failures reflect on them, asking their children to make up for all the things they never got to do. But inevitably, probably unintentionally, they give their children the mixed message "On the one hand, we're proud of you just as you are and we want you to end up somewhere where you'll be comfortable and happy. But at the same time, this is a once-in-a-lifetime opportunity for you to get a head start up the ladder of success. And after all we've done for you, is it too much to ask you to give us something to brag about when we get together with our friends?"

Again, I would emphasize my hesitancy to analyze the thought processes and emotional feelings of someone I never met, but if the pressure of getting into the best possible college was part of it, I wish someone would have shared with those grieving families Malcolm Gladwell's recent book *David and Goliath*, in which he brings evidence that people have happier lives and more successful careers if they are A students at a B-level college than if they are B students at an A-level college. Why would that be the case? Because you will have had the experience of success, of rising to the top, of being really good at what you do, and that confidence will serve you well in looking for a job, in looking for a life partner and in everything else you do. You might be better off in the long run, Gladwell insists, going to a college where you will still get a first-rate undergraduate education and have a better chance to impress one or more of your instructors as somebody special.

But if that were my whole response to the epidemic of people tempted to give up on life for fear that they are just not good enough, it might be a useful talk for a USY meeting but not for a Yom Kippur sermon. I think, though, that the plague that afflicts so many high school students, the fear of not being good enough, also afflicts those of us who are well beyond the teen-age years. It attacks us at our jobs, in our roles as hus-bands and wives, as parents. We compare ourselves to our neighbors, we compare ourselves to people we read about, and too many of us come away with the feeling that we don't measure up. The fear that we are just not good enough has the power to drain much of the joy and much of the enthusiasm from our lives at whatever age we find ourselves, and none of us deserve that.

How do you change that? How can you possibly change that? It comes down to the question of what we think life is really about. We have to choose between two paradigms, two metaphors for understanding life and finding a place for ourselves in it. That choice may not make a difference in what happens to us, but it will have a lot to say about how we feel regarding what happens to us. Here are the two possibilities. Do we see life as a competition, a contest with winners and losers, in which everyone who doesn't win loses? Do you believe that there is a limited supply of satisfaction in the world, like the limited number of places in a select college, or like a trip to the World Series or the Super Bowl that only two of the thirty or thirty-two major league teams will attain and everybody else goes home disappointed, so we have to hustle, even cheat if necessary to get our share before someone else can claim it? Is life, like sports, like poli-tics, a game of winners and losers? In politics, if you get 47 percent of the votes, you don't get 47 percent of the decision-making power. At best, you get your name in small print in the history books.

Or is there an alternative paradigm? Can we come to see life not as a competition but as a jigsaw puzzle, where the aim is to help everyone, including ourselves, find the right place for them, for us, so that the final result is something gratifying for everyone and nobody has to go home a loser? That is why—and every educator I know agrees with this statement—the annual *USNews* survey of the best colleges is a waste of paper published in an effort to sell magazines, because there is no such thing as the best college. It's like trying to identify the best ice-cream flavor. What is the perfect college for one young person might be a total mismatch for another. You don't want the *best* college for your eighteen-year-old son or daughter; you want the *right* college for them, the one where they will be able to flourish and find out who they are and what they are good at. You don't really want them spending those four years being reminded that they are not as good as most of the people around them. You shouldn't be looking for the best job as determined mostly by the salary level or by some abstract metric created by someone who has never met you. You shouldn't be looking for the best home to live in, even the best marriage partner. You should be looking for the *right* one, the best one for you even if it may not be the best for everyone.

I think of a man I knew some years ago—I met him after I endorsed a book he wrote. He wrote to me to thank me for the endorsement, and told me that he often found himself in Natick. His former wife and their children lived here, and he asked if we could meet for coffee sometime when he was in town. In the course of our getting to know each other, he told me the following story: He and a close friend were teaching English at one of the small colleges that grace the New England landscape. After a few years, they were up for tenure, and they were both denied. That's a way of saying they were fired. His friend refused to accept that, saying all he ever wanted to do in life was teach English at the college level. He appealed for a hearing. He threatened to sue the college. None of that helped. My friend, in contrast, wrote the administration a letter thanking them for releasing him from a job he was apparently not suited for, and went on to a second career at which he did very well. For him, teaching English was a good job but it was not the right job.

The paradigm of life as competition rather than cooperation, life as a contest rather than life as a jigsaw puzzle, not only creates many more losers than winners and increases the amount of unhappiness in the world (and who wants that?). It teaches us to see everybody else as a threat to our happiness, as people who want to get more of the limited amount of good things in life so there won't be any left for us. It's a system that leaves even the winners wondering what it is they have won and whether it was worth all the people they had to push aside to get there.

In S. Ansky's Yiddish classic, *The Dybbuk*, his drama of the supernatural, the central character is a wealthy man who, for reasons of greed, breaks off his daughter's engagement to his best friend's son, even though the couple is deeply in love and even though the two fathers, when they were boys growing up, swore that if one had a son and the other had a daughter, the two would marry. But now he has gone back on his word so that he can marry his daughter off to a wealthy merchant. The broken-hearted young man, in despair, kills himself, and his soul invades the soul of his former fiancée. That is the dybbuk, the ghost of a person that inhabits another person's body to set right an act of injustice. The girl's father, in desperation, arranges for an exorcism. It's at this point in the drama that a mysterious stranger shows up and engages the girl's father in conversation.

The stranger asks him to look out the window, asking "What do you see?" The father answers, "I see people." The stranger then takes him to the mirror. "Now what do you see?" "I see myself." "Isn't that interesting?" the stranger asks. "The window is made of glass, and the mirror is made of glass, but the glass in the mirror has had a thin coating of silver added to it. And as soon as the silver enters the picture, people can no longer see anyone else. They only see themselves."

When you see life as a competition for a limited supply of good things, not only is your perspective on other people distorted, not only do you set yourself up to be disappointed most of the time, even as all but one of the major league teams go home disappointed when the season is over. You pay the steep price of teaching yourself to see other people, people you probably have a lot in common with, as obstacles to your happiness, and in the process you miss out on some of the most gratifying experiences any of us will ever know: the experience of true friendship that is more about giving than getting, the experience of helping another person deal with his or her life. Can there be any better feeling in all the world than knowing that there is someone out there who is grateful for the fact that somebody like you exists in this world? I will confess that that has been the single most fulfilling aspect of my fifty-five years as a rabbi and of my thirty-two years as a best-selling author, not the fame and not the book sales but the knowledge that I and the religious traditions for which I speak have made some difficult moments more bearable for so many people.

That is why I was so disappointed recently to read the results of a national survey that found 80 percent of American young people rated personal success as more important to them than helping others. It saddened me that they have already learned to see life as a competition for a limited supply of satisfaction, a sorting out of people into winners and losers, with someone else's good fortune coming at your expense, feeling "that could have and should have been mine" rather than seeing life as an enterprise that we are all in together. The *Globe* reporter who covered the story tells of asking her sixteen-year-old son if he thought she appreciated his getting good grades in school more than she appreciated his habit of helping his grandmother get up and down the stairs. He replied, "That's a trick question, isn't it? Of course you do."

I remember Dennis Prager, speaking to this congregation years ago, challenging us: "How often have you praised your children for being smart, for getting good grades? And how often have you praised them for being kind? Yet aren't both of those equally important Jewish virtues?"

Our Jewish faith has one more item in its bag of tricks to cure us of the disease of fearing we are not good enough. It's called Yom Kippur. What is this day all about if not the inevitability of human failure and the assurance of divine forgiveness when we fail—from the opening words that come even before Kol Nidre, "*anu mattirim l'hitpallel im ha-avaryanim*, we reach out to include sinners in our congregation," to the repetition "*al het she-hattanu*, for the sin we have committed," it's an acknowledgment that all of us are less than perfect and that despite that fact, or perhaps because of that fact, all of us are welcome here. In the privacy of our hearts, during the moments of silent, individual contemplation of the liturgy, we admit to God "Yes, I messed up a lot of things this past year, things I knew at the time I should have done differently. I let people down, people I genuinely care about. I turned a deaf ear to people in need. All too often, I hid from the truth rather than admitting that I was wrong." And God says to us in reply, "Okay, now tell me something I didn't know. Of course you did those things, and so did every one of the hundreds of people sitting around you. You did those things, not because you're a bad person and not because you're a weak person, but because you're human." That's why we have this service every year and that's why so many people feel the need to be here for it. We welcome imperfect people, people who can be selfish, people who can be thoughtless to the service, because if we didn't do that, we'd never get a minyan.

Take my word for it: everyone sitting around you has had, and many may still have, those doubts as to whether they are good enough to handle a demanding job at work, good enough to raise a difficult child, good enough to close the gap between them and someone they genuinely care about. This is a service for imperfect people, to give them the feeling of being accepted in the sight of God and to give them the courage to step into a New Year. Ours is a religion for imperfect people, for people who, when we are being honest with ourselves, can't help wondering if we are good enough to be who we yearn to be. And the prayers of Yom Kippur say to them, "No, of course you're not going to do everything you would like to do, but you will do a lot of what you need to do, and you will do what you are capable of doing."

Still afraid that maybe you're not good enough? If you know that and you're still willing to try, don't be afraid. Yom Kippur would remind us that imperfect people are the only kind of people there are. And if that's good enough for God, it should be good enough for us as well.

L'shanah tovah tikatevu v'techatamu.

THE PURSUIT OF HOLINESS

The story is told of the British nobleman, a member of the House of Lords, who was leaving church one Sunday morning when the sermon had been about the sin of adultery, and was heard to remark, "I yield to no man in my admiration for the Church of England, but when it starts interfering with my private life, it goes too far."

In a somewhat similar vein, I yield to no man in my admiration for Thomas Jefferson. I think he was a great American, a towering intellect, a brilliant statesman, and an inspired writer. But he made one mistake 230 years ago for which we are still paying the price, and I hold him accountable for it. He wrote in the Declaration of Independence that "[all men] are endowed by their Creator with certain unalienable rights, that among these are Life, Liberty and the pursuit of Happiness."

Bad idea. For 230 years, Americans have been pursuing happiness and becoming increasingly frustrated when they could not achieve it. We have tried to find happiness by amassing wealth and learned that that didn't work. Whatever we had never seemed enough, and we had to neglect other priorities and learn to see other people as obstacles in the process. We tried to find happiness in the pursuit of pleasure and that didn't work either. We found fun, we found diversion, but never happiness. However rewarding the experience may have been, it was like a really good meal. It left you feeling satisfied for a few hours and then you were hungry again.

So let me try this morning to improve on Jefferson. Let me suggest that what God really blessed us with was life, liberty, and the pursuit of meaning. Happiness should never be our goal; it will always be a by-product, something that creeps into our lives while we are busy trying to live a life of meaning. The truth is, you can't pursue happiness. It has to pursue you. It has to sneak up on you while you are busy doing other things.

In a 1941 speech, American reporter and political commentator Walter Lippmann explored the relationship between happiness and desire. "People don't become happy by satisfying their desires," he said. Instead, happiness emerges from a belief system that gives order to a person's existence. According to Lippman, this sense of structure and discipline is more important than hunger, love, pleasure, fame, and even life itself.

Walter Lippmann was not a religious man, but what he was talking about that day is why we need religion. Religion is not a matter of obeying a lot of arbitrary laws to gain God's favor. It's just the opposite. It is a way of taking our wants, our needs, our cravings and putting them into an organized system, so that what we do makes sense at the deepest reaches of our souls.

In fact, if I dared to use a word that is too often mis-understood, I would say that the challenge God set for us was the pursuit of *holiness*.

Now, I know that "holiness" is a word that puts a lot of people off. It is at best something we can take in small doses. It speaks to us of a life out of the mainstream, a life of renunciation, Catholic nuns and Buddhist monks living lives of poverty and celibacy, and our instinctive response is "Thanks but no thanks."

But that gets it wrong. Holiness is not a renunciation of life; just the opposite. Holiness is life moving from black and white to color. It is life in high definition; everything becomes brighter and clearer, more interest-ing. The pursuit of holiness means *adding* a dimension to your life, not subtracting one, adding a dimension of meaning to what would otherwise be something none of us want to be, and that is "ordinary."

On the very first page of the Bible, when God cre-ates the world, He creates everything there is by com-mand, by fiat: "Let there be light, let there be grass and trees, let there be birds and fish and animals." But when it comes to creating the first human being, God doesn't just say "Let there be ..."; God fashions Adam out of earth and then breathes some of His own spirit into Adam, something God does for no other creature. Just before doing that, God says, *"Na-aseh Adam b'tzalmeynu,* Let us create a human being in our image." Us? Our? Whom is God talking to? I understand God to be speak-ing to the animals whom He has created in the verse immediately before that. I understand God to be say-ing to the animals as the last step in the evolutionary process, "Now let's come up with something unique: a creature that will be a combination of you and Me. It will be a physical being with physical needs, but it will have My breath, My spirit in it."

The human capacity for holiness reflects that uniqueness, the quality that makes us more interesting, more unpredictable than other animals, the ability that only we and God have to take something ordinary and make it special. And the pursuit of holiness means that, just as we go to school to develop our intellectual potential, just as we take piano lessons to develop our musical potential and go to the gym to develop our athletic potential, we turn to religion to develop our potential for holiness, the part of us that lets us rise above the animal level and be a little bit like God.

For much of recent Jewish history, we have tried to get people to be Jewishly observant for all the wrong reasons. Sometimes we urged people to follow Jewish laws and practices for God's sake, a way of doing something for God, and most of you were perceptive enough to figure out that God would probably manage to do just fine without us if He had to. Sometimes we told people, "This is the will of God and if you do these things, God will like you better." And a lot of people lived traditional Jewish lives on that basis and then got very upset when it seemed that God had defaulted on His part of the bargain. I have had countless people say to me, "If God could let this happen to my family, what good did all that coming to shul do me?" Now, I happen to believe there is an answer to that question. Did you read about the experiment a few months ago with two groups of postsurgical hospital patients? One group was prayed for, the other wasn't, and it didn't seem to make any difference in the time or nature of their recovery. When I was interviewed about it on CNN, I said, "God's job is not to make sick people healthy. That's the doctor's job. God's job is to make sick people brave."

But that's not the point. The point is that when God laid down the rules of the Torah, there was no promise of health and prosperity if we followed them. What there was, was a promise of holiness, that we would be a special people, a holy people. So this morning, I would like to give you a new way of looking at the ingredients of a Jewish life, based not so much on where these laws come from as on what they lead to.

For example, it should be clear to us that keeping kosher has little or nothing to do with health. I remember when I first came to Natick forty years ago, one member of the congregation explained to me that the Jewish dietary laws were based on obsolete notions of how meat and milk interacted in the stomach, ideas we now know are not true. Another shared his theory that they had to do with the lack of refrigeration in the Sinai desert. But the dietary laws never claimed to be about health. And they never claimed to be about teaching self-control, as you can verify at the next Jewish wedding you go to as you watch people fortify themselves with hors oeuvres lest they starve to death before dinner is served.

What the Jewish dietary law code is about is an absolutely brilliant, inspired way of introducing holiness into the act of eating, elevating it from something we share with animals to something that connects us to God by introducing into the act of eating concepts of permitted and forbidden. Animals eat anything that suits them; human beings, and only human beings, have the unique capacity to say No to certain foods, not because the food is spoiled and not because it contains trans fats or too many calories, but because they have voluntarily pledged themselves to a system that says certain foods are out of bounds, as a way of making the act of eating a mindful one and not just a matter of appetite.

There is a Jewish law that I suspect most of you have never heard of and few of you observe. I don't observe it, though I'd probably be better off if I did. Most Orthodox Jews don't observe it. What is it? According to the Talmud, you are not supposed to eat standing up. The Talmud says that horses eat standing up. Animals eat standing up. People sit down and make the process of taking in food a mindful one.

This is the genius of the Jewish dietary code. We don't teach people that the needs of the body are repulsive, corrupt, a concession to human weakness. We bring holiness into our meals the way we bring holiness into our sexual lives, not by abstaining but by imposing rules of permitted and forbidden on what is for all other creatures a matter of instinct.

If there are people here this morning who have never considered keeping kosher because you assumed it was based on obsolete pseudoscience but you are intrigued at the prospect of using it to turn breakfast, lunch, and dinner into mindful, uniquely human experiences rather than just another occasion to refuel your corporeal gas tank, I hope you will use the New Year to make a New Start. You don't have to go whole hog (or in this case, whole no-hog). There are intermediate steps you can take.

In much the same way, I think we have totally mishandled the way we have urged people to keep the Sabbath. We have said to them, "On Shabbat, it is forbidden to turn on lights, it is forbidden to spend money, it is forbidden to drive to visit relatives. Don't do a lot of things you might enjoy doing. And the reason is to celebrate the fact that you have been liberated from slavery." All these rules and prohibitions to make the point that you're not a slave? Am I missing something?

Suppose instead of giving you rules, a long list of Don'ts, suppose we said to you, "All week long, you are defined by your work, by what you earn and what you spend. You deserve a day on which you define yourself by who you are and not what you earn. Suppose we said to you, "All week long, you are a slave to a schedule. How often in an average day do you check your watch to make sure you're not running late? Can you even keep track of the number of times? You deserve a day in which the concept of running late does not exist, a day when you will tell time not by looking at your watch but by following the course of the sun across the sky."

Just as the system of keeping kosher makes us different from animals, puts us in touch with the breath of God inside us, by the way we relate to food, Shabbat makes us different from animals in the way we relate to time. Animals are controlled by time. Some are active in daylight, others are nocturnal. Some are active year-round, others hibernate in winter. But they have no choice in the matter. The clock and the calendar even tell them when to mate and when to bear their young. Only human beings can shape time to our purposes. Only we can arbitrarily take a day—a birthday, an anniversary, a holiday—and for no reason except our choosing, we can make that day feel special.

Do you realize that for 98 percent of Americans, and for 99.9 percent of the human race, there is nothing special about today? But for us, it is an experience of holiness, a time to stand before God and come to see ourselves as God sees us, and it is special only because we chose to make it special.

You understand that a day, a month, a year are astronomical events. They have to do with the earth's path around the sun and the moon's course around the earth. They would happen even if there were no human being on the planet. But a week is a human invention, a way of expressing our power to define time, and Shabbat, a day of liberation from the tyranny of time, is the great symbol of that.

Again, as with the dietary laws, once you buy into the concept, you will find your own way to live it, remembering only that some of the attractions of getting and spending, of filling every hour of the day with obligations, the tar pit we live in during the week, can be every bit as seductive as a cheeseburger. I would offer two pieces of advice: First, I would start by giving the tradition the benefit of the doubt. Start with it and work your way down rather than start with nothing and work your way up. Second, it is a lot easier to make Shabbat special in a community, in the company of other people who are striving to do the same.

There is one more dimension worth mentioning. When Hitler destroyed European Jewry, he not only killed people; in six years, he destroyed a civilization that had taken a thousand years to create. He destroyed centers of learning and fountains of holiness that the Jewish world of Europe represented. In the sixty years since the end of World War II, we have replaced the learning. American Jewry has done an astonishing job of producing Jewish scholars, writing serious Jewish books of a kind that did not exist until a few years ago, establishing departments of Jewish studies at countless universities. It has been a remarkable achievement. But we haven't replaced the holiness that died with the Jews of Europe. We have filled the intellectual vacuum the Holocaust created, but there is still a holiness deficit in the world, and the world is a less decent place than it was a century ago because of it. This then becomes our sacred task as Jews, for our sakes, for the world's sake. This is how you assure yourself that your life has meaning: add to the store of holiness in a world that is suffering from a lack of holiness because it doesn't understand as our Jewish tradition has taught us to understand what holiness is all about.

What will it do for us? It will put you in touch with a part of yourself that has been lying dormant for all these years, and it may turn out that that was what you've been missing. It is the most distinctively human part of you, the part of you that is most like God and least like all those other creatures on earth. When you relate humanly to food by making each mealtime a visit with God, when you relate humanly to time by shaping one day a week to what *you* need rather than what others need from you, when you relate humanly to your possessions by giving charity and discovering that it doesn't hurt, then you will be well on your way to achieving the real goal of your life—the pursuit of holiness, the pursuit of fulfilled human potential—and the happiness that has been searching for you all these years will finally find you.

PLAYING BY THE RULES

Let me tell you a story. It's a story attributed to the saintly Hassidic master Levi Yitzchok of Berditchev. It seems that a young man from Berditchev, to the embarrassment of his family, went off in a bad direction. He became a criminal, a pickpocket, stealing from neighbors, robbing people, showing no respect for the law or for other people's property. The young man died shortly after Rosh HaShanah, and as one would expect, he went to hell as a punishment for the life he had led. When he arrived in hell during these days between Rosh HaShanah and Yom Kippur, the first thing he saw was Satan putting the finishing touches on the dossier he was preparing to present to God on Yom Kippur, detailing all the sins of Jews throughout the world, every lie, every act of deceit or cruelty. It was a long and embarrassing document, and Satan was prepared to use it to convince God to inscribe all those less-than-perfect Jews for a year of misery and misfortune. At that point, the thief realized that this was the moment for which his entire life had been a preparation. While Satan's back was turned, he picked Satan's pocket, stole the dossier, and threw it into the fires of hell, destroying the evidence. At that moment, a band of angels flew down into hell, picked up the thief and carried him up to heaven.

I found that story in a book I read an advance copy of last year called *The Holy Thief*. It's the autobiography of a man who must be the most unusual Conservative rabbi in America. His name is Mark Borovitz. He lives in Los Angeles, and he spent most of his life either committing crimes or going to prison for his crimes, before a prison counselor straightened him out and put him on a path that ultimately led to rabbinical school. He now runs a combination synagogue and halfway house for habitual lawbreakers who are trying to go straight.

Mark Borovitz was a fourteen-year-old boy in Cleveland when his father died and his family had no way to pay its bills. When nothing else worked out, a family friend put him in touch with the Cleveland Mafia and he began selling stolen electronic goods. By his junior year in high school, he was spending his evenings serving as president of his synagogue's USY chapter and his afternoons earning $500 a week selling hijacked boom boxes and television sets to his high school classmates.

After high school, he branched out into stealing and forging checks. On a couple of occasions, he went into business selling cars and did not hesitate to cheat his partners as readily as he cheated his customers. He went to prison several times; at one point between sentences, he got married and had a daughter. But no matter how often he promised his family that he was going to stop, he kept going back to a life of crime, until finally a prison chaplain was able to get through to him.

I had occasion to be in Los Angeles shortly after I read Mark Borovitz's life story, so I called him up and invited him to have breakfast with me. I asked him, "Why does a person like you do what you did? You know it's a virtual certainty that sooner or later you'll be caught and go back to prison. You know you're hurting your family. You keep promising them that you'll change but you don't change. There is that one heartbreaking scene in your book where your fourteen-year-old daughter pleads with you not to do anything that would send you to prison again, and you swear to her that you won't. Then that same afternoon, you take money out of her college savings account to finance your gambling on football games. Doesn't it occur to a person that if he's clever enough to think up these elaborate schemes in the first place, he's probably clever enough to make a good living honestly, without the embarrassment and the prison time? Why does a person keep doing it?"

He looked at me and said, "It's really simple. When there is a fundamental emptiness inside you, there is something exhilarating about being able to say, 'The rules don't apply to me.'"

I said to him, "Of course; that makes a lot of sense. That explains the teenage girl who shoplifts even though she can afford to buy ten times over what she steals. That explains the man or woman who acquires a drug habit even though they don't really enjoy it and it takes all their money, but they love the feeling of doing something forbidden. That explains the husband who cheats on his wife. It's their way of quieting that nagging voice inside them that says to them, "You're nobody special," by letting them say, "I am special; the rules that apply to other people don't apply to me."

Why would King David, with a house overflowing with wives and concubines, covet the wife of one of his soldiers? It's not the money and it's not the sex. It's the exhilarating feeling of being able to say, "The rules don't apply to me."

So, would keeping kosher really help any of us? Maybe, maybe not. There are all too many instances of people who keep kosher and violate ethical standards in other areas. But think of it this way: I can imagine that every one of you will come to a moment in your life when your future happiness will depend on your saying No to temptation. It may be a lucrative but shady business deal. It may be an illicit sexual involvement. It may be an invitation to spend money you don't have on some attractive luxury. Whatever the circumstance, you'll know it's wrong, you'll know it has the potential to seriously mess up your life. But it will be very tempting. Now, if that is the first time in your life that you have to say No to temptation, what are the chances that you'll get it right the first time, with your future happiness depending on it? And what are the chances that you'll give in to the attraction of placing yourself above the rules? But if you have spent your whole life saying No to tempting things, if you have been doing things to make yourself strong in the behavioral sphere the way people who go to the gym lift weights to make themselves strong physically, a process incidentally known as "resistance training," doesn't that improve your chances of getting it right?

And what is Yom Kippur if not a celebration of our ability to say No to things that tempt us the other 364 days of the year? Remember what Rabbi Borovitz said to me: it's the person who is lacking something inside who needs to give his self-esteem a boost by deciding that the rules don't apply to him. The really superior athlete enjoys the feeling of being able to win without cheating. It's the athlete who is afraid he's not good enough who feels he has to cheat to compete. The really good student takes pleasure in doing her homework herself, without having to ask for help or peek at the answers in the back of the book. And the person who takes Yom Kippur seriously enough to do it right emerges at nightfall feeling cleansed and strengthened, with a new appreciation of his or her willpower. We will walk out of here tomorrow night saying to ourselves, "Hey, I just found out how strong I can be."

I want to move this discussion to another level by introducing you to a verse from the Torah, from the Book of Leviticus, and I'm going to suggest that this may be the first time in history that this verse has been used as the basis for a High Holy Day sermon. It comes from chapter 19 of Leviticus, the chapter known as the Holiness Code because it begins with the command "You shall be holy for I the Lord your God am holy," and then it spells out several dozen ways of introducing holiness into our lives. It's a strange blend of obligations and prohibitions. It tells us to honor our parents and show respect to the elderly and the handicapped. It forbids revenge and getting even. It commands us to leave a corner of our field unharvested, for the poor to come and help themselves to it. It contains the verse "You shall love your neighbor as yourself." But it also has some far-out ritual laws, like the command that an animal sacrifice brought in celebration of something must be eaten entirely on that day, with no leftovers, or the prohibition of wearing clothing made of two kinds of material, one of animal origin, one of plant origin.

Then in the middle of the chapter, we read, "When you enter the land and plant any tree for fruit, you shall regard its fruit as forbidden. Three years it shall be forbidden to you, not to be eaten." What are we to make of that law? I always understood it to be based on the assumption that for the first few years of a fruit tree's life the fruits are inedible until the tree matures. The purpose of the law is not to tell people not to eat unripe fruit; they could have figured that out for themselves. The purpose, I thought, was to exempt the fruit of the first three years from being brought to the altar as part of the offering of first fruits every spring. To offer unripe, inedible fruit on the altar would be like bringing a lame or sick animal for a sacrifice. It's not worth anything to you, so it's no sacrifice. That's how I always understood it, and when I wrote the *Etz Hayim* commentary on the Torah that we and other Conservative synagogues use on Shabbat, that was how I explained it.

But last year I read a book by my classmate Professor Jack Neusner, who is probably our generation's greatest authority on the Talmud. Commenting on this verse as part of an examination of the theology implicit in biblical and rabbinic law, Neusner picks up on something that I had never noticed: the phrase "forbidden fruit."

Did this remind us of anything? Of course! Adam and Eve in the Garden of Eden.

Neusner's dramatically bold interpretation of this verse would suggest that something very unfortunate happened in the world when Adam and Eve could not keep their hands off the fruit of the Tree of Knowledge. As a result of what they did, their descendants—that is to say, all of us—grew up as people who would have trouble with self-control, people who could not be counted on to play by the rules, people who will cheat if that's what they have to do to win, people who could not reliably say No to temptation, and the world has been a mess ever since because of it. When God commands the Jewish people to be holy, and part of that holiness involves what we eat and what we don't eat, what He is doing is challenging us to atone for the sin of Adam and Eve who could not say No to temptation. He is challenging us *to redeem the world* by practicing self-restraint, by learning to say No. That is the essence of holiness. When we fast on Yom Kippur, when we come out of this day with a new resolve to live by Jewish standards, we atone for that Original Sin and make this truly a Day of Atonement.

Neusner's theory offers a fascinating contrast to standard Christian theology, and I want to choose my words carefully here because I don't want to be unfair to Christianity. Christianity says that because human beings are unable to resist temptation, unable to say No to what they know is wrong, we have estranged ourselves from God, and the only way to bridge that gap is for God to make a supreme personal sacrifice. We flawed human beings can't bridge the gap by our own efforts.

Judaism says that because human beings are unable to resist temptation, unable to say No to what they know is wrong, we have estranged ourselves from God. So God says to us, "You broke it; you fix it. Show Me, by acts of self-restraint in your eating, in your speech, in your sexual behavior, in the way you earn and spend money, show Me that you've grown up and have learned to say No."

Think about that for a moment. Do you realize what an audacious statement that is? It's saying that, when we take Yom Kippur seriously, when we take the rules of Judaism seriously, when we take our own lives seriously, *we redeem the world from brokenness.* It's not just a matter of being good Jews and pleasing God. It's not even solely a matter of personal morality. It's a challenge to the Jewish people, by our behavior, to repair the breach between God and the entire human race.

I would remind you of what Rabbi Borovitz told me that morning in Los Angeles. It's the people who feel empty inside, people whose lives are devoid of meaning, who need to boost their egos by saying, "I don't have to live by the rules. The rules don't apply to me." When your teenage or adult children say to you, "Why should being Jewish be important to me?" and you tell them about a hundred generations of ancestors who sacrificed so much to preserve their Jewish identity and they tell you that's ancient history, and you warn them about anti-Semitism and they respond, "Maybe when you were growing up, but I've never had problems with my non-Jewish friends," maybe you could try telling them that in some mysterious way that we can't understand, by some process that doesn't follow the laws of physics or politics, the world needs the Jewish people in order to fix what is broken in the world. The world needs Jews who take their Jewishness seriously, to redeem it from the misbehavior of all those people who think only about themselves. That would be the one thing that persuades God to go on tolerating this messed-up world.

A young woman said to me at one of my lectures, "To me, Judaism is not dietary laws and going to synagogue. To me, Judaism is *tikkun olam*, social action, doing things for other people to make the world better. Everything else is just a distraction from that." I said to her, "Great, I'm all in favor of tikkun olam, but let's try to understand what that means. In Jewish theology, tikkun olam means fixing what is broken in the world. And what is broken in the world is not just economic oppression. What's broken in the world is the difficulty people have seeing themselves as human beings who are capable of holiness. Tikkun olam has to mean more than serving meals to people with AIDS and picketing Wal-Mart. Tikkun olam, literally "repairing the world," means undoing the sin of Adam and Eve by becoming models of self-restraint as well as models of caring and generosity, self-restraint in the way you eat and drink and dress and speak, not just for your sake so you don't mess up your life by giving in to temptations, not just for God's sake; God will be just fine whether you live by the Torah or not, but for the world's sake, so that our saying No to temptation will move God to say Yes to letting the world continue to exist, because if there is no holiness in the world, what does God need a world for?

Is it realistic to believe that this tiny sliver of the world's population who are Jewish can repair the damage done by the other six billion humans? I wouldn't dare to suggest it, except that it has happened before. One man, Abraham, with his wife and son, pledged themselves to a new understanding of God, and the rest of the world fell in line.

A few thousand people standing at Sinai went on to teach the world about a God who demanded righteous behavior and not only sacrifice and blind obedience. We gave the world the Ten Commandments, the psalms, and the prophets, and three thousand years later, a majority of the human race looks at issues of morality through Jewish lenses. The rich culture of Europe in the first third of the twentieth century, unparalleled creativity in music, art, theater and literature, was overwhelmingly the work of a few dozen Jews living in Berlin, Prague, Paris, and Vienna who saw the world differently than their neighbors did. Jews have been such a factor in the cultural and spiritual life of America—shaping the film and television industries, teaching at the best universities, writing and publishing books, enriching medicine, law, and commerce—hardly anyone believes that we are less than 2 percent of the American population. How could that be when everyone's doctor, lawyer, accountant or favorite newspaper columnist is Jewish? And when you realize that all of us without exception think about the world around us and the world inside us differently than people did 150 years ago because of two Jews, Albert Einstein and Sigmund Freud, why shouldn't we believe that we have the ability to make the world a different place?

The problem is, I'm sorry to have to say, that when people think about what it means to be Jewish in America today, I'm not sure that saying No to temptation is the first thing that comes to mind. The American Jewish community has too often defined itself by excess, by extravagance. We have insisted that we don't need rules. We don't need to give anything up. We can be Jewish without being religious, because Jewishness was a matter of ancestry, of who your grandparents were rather than what your values are, memories of holiness rather than experiences of holiness. And so you get the Jackie Masons and the Woody Allens for whom Judaism is something funny, something to make jokes about, not something redemptive, and we wonder why our children don't take their Jewishness seriously.

Yes, we are still more charitable than any other segment of the population and we still value education more than any subset of our neighbors. But there was a time when we cherished those things but we also had a talent for holiness, when we knew how to sanctify time, how to turn our kitchen tables into altars, how to guard our tongues from profanity and malicious gossip, and I fear we've lost it. And because we've lost it, because we have shirked our unique responsibility, the world we live in remains a broken place, an unredeemed place, a world in which it is often hard to find God.

The world we live in is a mess because people have forgotten the art of holiness, because we have forgotten that the essence of holiness, from the pages of Leviticus to the breakfast we'll choose not to have on Yom Kippur, the essence of holiness, of genuine tikkun olam, is playing by the rules, saying No to things that tempt us, even as we sanctify Yom Kippur by overruling our hunger, even as we are summoned to sanctify the Sabbath by liberating ourselves from the stressful world of making and spending money, even as we are enjoined to sanctify the most powerful instinct of all, the sexual drive, not with celibacy but with chuppah and kiddushin, with a marriage ceremony.

The world is starved for holiness. The world is broken for lack of holiness. It's hard to find God in a world deprived of self-restraint. And we, the people who first taught the world what it means to be a holy people, we have the power and we have the sacred obligation to make the world whole again. May this coming year see us all blessed with life, with health, with material success, but more than anything else, for our sakes and for the world's sake, may this coming year see us blessed with lives of holiness.

MEN ARE NOT MACHINES

It happens sometimes that one small incident manages to capture in itself a whole trend that has been going on for some time, and comes to symbolize that trend, so that something you've been thinking about abstractly becomes vividly real. Something like that happened to me about a year and a half ago. My wife's nephew was about to be graduated from Rensselaer Polytech in Troy, New York, and we went up to Troy to be with him. He was showing us around the campus, and after a series of sleek modern laboratories, libraries, and lecture halls, we came to an old stone building with Gothic arches and stained glass windows. I said to my nephew, "Don't tell me, let me guess. I bet this is the chapel." He said, "It used to be. It's now the computer center."

To me, that seemed to epitomize what has been happening in American society, computer centers where churches used to be. When *Time* magazine last January chose the home computer as its Man of the Year, it was their way of saying that no human being, not even the human beings who designed and built the computer, had shaped our lives in 1982 as much as those machines had.

What does it mean when we turn college chapels into computer centers, and choose a machine as Man of the Year? For most of human history, the most important moral question that religion could ask was "How is a human being different from an animal?" And most religious teaching was designed to make men more than animals, to teach us self-restraint, control of our instincts, of hunger and lust and anger. Religion strove to teach us to sanctify our power of speech, to pray and to bless, because that was something that human beings could do and animals could not.

For three thousand years, religion has been saying to people, "These are the skills you have to practice, these are the laws you have to obey, so that you can be a mensch and not an animal." Our myths, our fables, our fairy tales, and too often our history spoke to us about the thin line that divided men from beasts, and how easily that line could be crossed.

But it may be that the 1980s represent a turning point in human moral history, a time when the fundamental question is no longer "What does a it mean to be human, not an animal?" but "What does it mean to be human and not a machine?" This is how religion changes, not by coming up with newer and better answers than our forefathers had, but by realizing that the world is asking us new and different questions.

Human beings are turned into machines when we see them as replaceable, interchangeable, when we start to think that we can take one person out of a system and put in another, newer, cheaper, improved model without doing harm either to the system or to the people involved. Human beings are turned into machines when we define ourselves in terms of what we do rather than who we are. Some of you will remember that last year at this time, I pointed out that traditional societies honored the elderly because they were wise, and modern societies become impatient with the elderly because they're not productive.

Man becomes more like a machine when he comes alive on Monday mornings and he goes back to work—it's revealing that the phrase we use for this is that his work "turns him on"—and he doesn't know what to do with himself when he's home with his family on the weekend.

When we forget how to feel, when we forget how to care, when we forget how to celebrate, we teeter on the edge of losing our human uniqueness and becoming like the machines that were designed to serve us and have become instead our masters and our models. That's why it becomes so urgent for us, as we begin a New Year, to find answers to a question that we never had to ask before: "What are the things that make us human beings and not machines?"

How am I different from my computer? It can do a lot of things faster and more accurately than I can, but that's only a difference of degree, not of innate nature. After all, one person can run a lot faster, read a lot faster, multiply a lot faster than another, but they're both human beings. What are the essential differences?

When people first began to become aware of computers, I remember asking an engineer friend of mine,

"Is there anything that people can do that computers can't?" and he answered, "Sure, they can make mistakes". And that's not necessarily so terrible. There is something kind of endearing, something quite essentially human about the fact that we're not perfect, we make mistakes. A teacher of mine, a specialist in medieval Jewish philosophy, was telling us once of discovering a hitherto unknown essay on philosophy by Maimonides, the great Jewish thinker who lived in the twelfth century. Some scholars doubted its authenticity because in several places the essay contradicted what Maimonides had written in his great work, *The Guide for the Perplexed.* But my teacher said, on the contrary, that was the proof that it was genuine. Had it agreed with other writings in every detail, he would have suspected that it was the work of a forger, copying from Maimonides's published writings. But Maimonides was a human being, given to moods and changes like the rest of us. Because it was inconsistent, he was convinced that it was genuine.

Human beings are inconsistent. We're not machines. We feel differently one day than we did a few days earlier, and so we see things differently. We grow, we change, we have our good and bad days. And certainly, one of the messages of the High Holy Day liturgy is that we can't expect people to be anything other than human. We have to allow for mistakes; we can't demand perfection from ourselves or from anyone else. Moreover, when something goes wrong while I'm running my computer (and it's never entirely clear if it's my fault or the machine's fault; I used to think that machines never made mistakes, only the people operating them did, but

I've had so many mistakes blamed on computer break-
down that I'm not sure anymore). When something goes
wrong, my computer takes it all in stride, but I get upset.
I get angry; that's the human being in me coming out.

Anger can be a pretty petty emotion. It can be
summoned forth by all sorts of unworthy occasions.
But anger doesn't have to be petty. It can verge on the
sublime. Becoming angry can be a way of saying, "This
isn't the way things ought to be; they ought to be better,
fairer, less painful." Anger can be a way of saying that,
because we are human, we can not only see things as
they are, we can see how they ought to be, as they would
be in a more perfect world, and the gap between the
two, between what is and what should be, is what bothers us.

Trivial anger has caused dishes to be shattered,
bones to be broken, friendships to be ended. But good,
honest, righteous anger has been used to make some
very good things happen. We changed the laws in this
country that permitted segregation of the races because
enough people got angry. We supported our government in the war against Hitler, and forced it to recon-
sider the war in Vietnam, because in both cases we got
angry. We improved the lot of the poor, the elderly, the
neglected because instead of simply, dispassionately col-
lecting information about them as a computer would,
we read the stories and we got angry.

I remember my teacher Professor Heschel saying
once that if Plato had ever read the Bible, he would
have been embarrassed by the way in which it describes
God—a God who denounces liars and robbers, who gets

angry if widows and orphans are denied their rights. How petty, Plato would say, how trivial. God should really be above such things. He should be concerned with the *idea* of Justice, not with one accident, one widow, one child. For Plato, for Aristotle, God is the Unmoved Mover, said Heschel, but for Amos and Isaiah, God is not unmoved. He is very easily moved; He is moved by suffering, by unfairness. In the seventeenth century, Spinoza proved logically that it was impossible for God to get angry, because anger is a passion, and passion represents change and God can't change, because if He changed, He would either be perfect before the change but not after, or else the other way around. But in the Bible, God often gets angry, because sometimes anger is the only appropriate response to the way His creation is being defiled. God gets angry with a sense of righteousness that is more compelling than Spinoza's logic.

And really, what is the alternative? The alternative to getting angry is apathy, not caring, not summoning up an emotional response to the wrong things that happen. For the Jew, God is not simply a computer, making sure the sun rises and the seasons change on schedule. God is a God who cares, and we are human beings fashioned in His image, and not mere machines, when we care too.

If you read about people starving, children going hungry, and you don't get upset, if you just process the information, add it to your store of knowledge, then you're more like a computer and less than a complete human being. When we get so used to crime and fraud and political corruption that it doesn't bother us anymore, when we can only see what is and no longer simultaneously have a vision of what should be, then one of the precious dimensions of what makes us human is in danger of being lost.

I mentioned recently after a taping of *Topic: Religion*, the interfaith radio show I used to do every week, that I was going to be speaking today on the issues of what makes us, as human beings, different from computers, Sister Mary Hennessey, the Roman Catholic nun of the program, said without a moment's hesitation. "Compassion." That's what makes us human. Not intelligence; machines can come pretty close to having that. Not imagination or moral awareness; those come later. But compassion, the people open to feeling the anguish of another person's pain. A lot of people have trouble with that. They are more comfortable dealing with machines, with objects, because they don't make any emotional demands on us. Dealing with another person can be very risky.

I don't mean to sound as if I'm name-dropping, but the last time I was on the *Today* show, Jane Pauley asked me what I had learned from the letters and phone calls my book had prompted. Was I picking up any trend in human anguish? At first, I didn't know what to make of her question. I almost thought she was asking me to identify the coming trend in suffering; you know, "We were the first one on our block to have herpes, we were anorexic before anybody else had ever heard of it. What this year's 'in' disease?" Then I thought of a pattern I had noticed that surprised me. I told her I had received perhaps twenty-five letters from women who wrote to tell me that, when they had gotten sick or had a child who was seriously ill, their husbands left them. My impression was that these men didn't leave their families because they were callous, unfeeling people. Just the opposite—they left because they felt too deeply. They hurt very much for their wife or child, and they didn't know how to handle the pain, so they ran away from it.

Our culture is unfair to women in many ways, but it's unfair to men in at least one big way: it teaches us that "real men don't cry," that it is unmanly to feel pain or fear or any other emotion. It inundates us with John Wayne or Gary Cooper movies, till we learn not to let anything get to us. Typically, in about half of the funerals at which I officiate, there will be one woman in her seventies crying and shouting at the top of her voice, "Why? Why did it have to happen? He was so good. Why did he have to die?" And there will be a man in his forties looking very annoyed and uncomfortable, and saying, "Can't somebody make her shut up? Can't somebody give her a sedative or something?" as if there were something wrong with crying and feeling sad at a funeral.

I sometimes think this is why professional sports is so important in America. It's the one place where a man can get emotionally involved, where he can cry and cheer and groan, without having his manliness called into question.

We're evolving a new type of human being in this technological age, one who has no trouble relating to other people financially, who has no trouble communicating with people physically, but who doesn't know how to get involved with people emotionally. We say to our children, as we say to our husbands and wives, "You want to have something, I'll buy it for you, no matter how expensive. You need to get somewhere, I'll drive you, no matter how inconvenient, because I understand what it means to spend time and money. But when you ask me to *care* about you, to listen to you, not only to understand the words but to understand the spaces between the words, to know where you hurt and what to do about it, that I don't understand. I don't even know what hurts *me*; how can I know what hurts you?" No wonder we're afraid of being replaced by robots.

But if our goal is to be human, to *live* and not simply to function, then we have to focus ourselves beyond what we're comfortable with, and learn skills that don't come easily to us. We have to summon up the courage to walk out into a very dangerous world without the suits of armor we're used to wearing, and if we're hurt, we'll hurt, and if we bleed, we bleed. But only when we take off the armor does it become possible for us to get close to other people. With the armor on, we're prepared to see other people in our world as enemies, as threats, as competitors, but it's harder to accept them as friends.

Maybe in the same way that religion in its earlier incarnation gave us mitzvoth of self-control—don't eat that food, don't give in to other natural instincts—we today need to be given the mitzvoth of feeling: give charity to the needy even though you don't feel like it; reach out emotionally to someone even if it's scary at first: pay the condolence call, visit the friend in the hospital; speak out about something that you feel isn't right—so that we regain some of the human traits we're in danger of losing.

It's a brand-new year, and it's up to us to decide what to do with it. Habits of the past don't count. We can see these days—today and tomorrow and next Saturday—as an obligation to be checked off; do it and get it over with, because that's what is expected of a Jew. Or we can see them as they used to be seen, as *Yamim Noraim*, as Days of Awe, days when the prayers move and frighten and exalt people.

You know, people used to cry on Rosh HaShanah. They cried not just because they were afraid of dying, but because the issues of the High Holy Days moved them to tears. They cried when they realized how they had hurt and let down people they loved. They cried when they remembered promises they had made and broke, when they reflected on the uncertainty of life, when they pondered the vulnerability that comes with being a year older.

Why don't we cry today? Why don't we let those questions get to us as they got to our grandparents? Is it because we're so much more secure, so much more self-confident than they were? Or is it because we're so self-conscious, so afraid of letting our guard down, of exposing any weakness, that we hide our fears and our tears even from ourselves? To come to shul on Rosh HaShanah and not admit that we're afraid, not admit that some memories of last year embarrass us, is like going to the doctor and lying to him about how you feel so that he'll think you're healthy, and then wondering when you get home why you don't feel better.

Are we in fact human beings and not elaborate machines? Then let us locate our humanity in our capacity to get upset when reality falls short of what it might be or should be. Let us run the risk of hurting and bleeding when we venture out of our shells and connect our lives to the lives of others.

And let us locate our humanity in one place as well: in our ability to grow and change, to surprise ourselves and to surpass ourselves. Only human beings can do that. Words can change us—words of prayer, words of affection and encouragement—because we're human. Encounters with other people can change us because we're human. Disappointment with what last year had been and a vision of what the New Year might be can change us and make us live our lives differently. This is what it means to begin a New Year. It means our coming to shul, not simply to recite the prayers but to confront them, to respond to them, to become different people because we have read them, to walk out of here this morning saying, "The story of the New Year will not be the story of what happened to me. It will be the story of what I decide to be, of what I choose, of what I can make happen."

KNOWING OUR OWN
STRENGTH

I don't know how you reacted to the Rededication Weekend for the Statue of Liberty last Fourth of July, but I loved it. I mean, what better way to celebrate America as a land of opportunity for all than to have two hundred Elvis Presley look-alikes singing together? You felt that must have been what the poet Emma Lazarus had in mind when she wrote about "The wretched refuse of your teeming shore."

But seriously, I was very moved by the ceremonies, as an American and as a Jew. I think the Statue of Liberty, placed in New York harbor in 1886, the time and place that saw the greatest Jewish immigration to these shores, has always meant something special to the American Jew. It welcomed my parents when they came from Eastern Europe in the early years of the century, and I suspect it was there to greet the parents and grandparents of many of you. And even for those of us whose families came to those shores before 1886 or arrived at ports of entry other than New York City, I think the Statue of Liberty meant something special for us and our families. It was America's official answer to a question that almost no American Jew can avoid asking, "Do we really belong here?"

Whether we studied Jewish history covering the two thousand years of the Diaspora or whether we had heard stories of discrimination from our parents and grandparents, or even if we had been called names on our way home from school or overheard jokes at our expense, we knew how fragile and insecure a Jewish minority had been wherever our people had lived.

But the Statue of Liberty represented the promise that American would be different, that even if there were individual bigots and bullies, the official American position was that America welcomed immigrants, that all who came in search of freedom would be accepted here. "Do we really belong here?" That's a much older Jewish question than we realize. It goes beyond the immigration from Europe, even beyond the destruction of the Temple and dispersion of the Jews nineteen centuries ago. It goes back to the earliest days of the Jewish people, to Abraham. In a passage that comes immediately after the chapter we read on Rosh HaShanah, Abraham's wife Sarah dies and he has to arrange for a burial plot for her. He says to his Canaanite neighbors in whose midst he has lived for years, *"ger v'toshav anochi imachem*, I am a stranger and a resident in your midst. Will you help me buy the Cave of Machpela from its current owner?" The rabbis comment on those words that Abraham was not sure whether he was a *toshav*, a full-fledged resident of the community after all the years he had lived there, or whether he was a *ger*, a stranger among them. Was he one of them because he had lived there so long, because he had contributed so much to the community, even though his ways and beliefs were different, or despite all that, did they persist in seeing him as a stranger?

It sounds a lot like the ambivalence I have heard from members of this congregation, and from other American Jews, about running for public office or being conspicuous in other ways. Are we really fully accepted; are we just like anybody else? Or is there something fragile and tentative about the status we have achieved? Do we have to watch our step and be careful not to offend, not to be too conspicuous? No Protestants reacted to James Walker and Jerry Whitworth getting caught spying for the Russians the way so many Jews reacted to Jonathan Pollard being caught spying for Israel. It's like the ambivalence we feel when a Pat Robertson or one of the other television preachers calls on Americans to make the United States a Christian nation. Like Abraham, we've been here a long time. We've paid our dues; we've served in the armed forces. And we are still not sure whether we are really fully welcome.

If you are surprised that Abraham was already asking that question four thousand years ago, you'll be even more surprised at the answer his Canaanite neighbors gave him. They didn't say, "You're welcome here because we are very generous about tolerating minorities." They didn't say, "Hey, people are all the same; we don't care what a man believes as long as he's a goodneighbor. They said "*N'si Elohim atta b'tocheinu,* You are God's representative in our midst." They said, "We're grateful that you are here, because you make our community a different community by your presence, because you have brought God into our midst."

There is a phenomenon, a rather widespread psychological phenomenon, of people not know their own strength, of feeling weak and vulnerable because they are so familiar with their faults and weaknesses, but have no idea how powerful they really are. Friends of mine who are therapists, for example, will describe a young woman in treatment who will complain constantly that she can't be happy because her mother tyrannizes her. Her mother is always putting her down; she makes plans and her mother forces her to change them. Her mother is always making her feel guilty. She paints this portrait of her mother as an ogre, a domineering tyrant who won't let her grow up and be her own person. Then one day the therapist gets to meet the mother, and she turns out to be a frail, sick old lady, in no shape to tyrannize anyone, desperately afraid of being abandoned and left along in her old age. If she won't let go, it's not because she wants to control. It's because she is afraid that if she doesn't clutch and hold on, her daughter who has so many more interesting things to do will leave her to fend for herself. The mother sees only her own weaknesses and her daughter's power. She doesn't realize that, old and feeble as she may be, she still has the power to turn her daughter into a little girl again, anxious for her approval. The daughter sees only her own weakness, and she doesn't realize how helpless her mother is against her power to stay away and keep the grandchildren at a distance. And what the therapist has to do is bring each of them to appreciate her own power, so that she will feel less threatened by the strength of the other.

To be a Jew is to be painfully aware of the volcano of anti-Semitism simmering just below the surface of American life. The reference to the Jew as villain is never far out of reach. To be a Jew in American is to be conscious of the fact that there are not many really good jobs or really good colleges, and if you are Jewish, there will always be extra barriers placed between you and them. To be a Jew is to realize the insecurity of the American Jew. We feel insecure, we act insecure, sometimes because we don't know our own strength. Like Abraham, we don't know if we are being tolerated or if we have actually gained acceptance and equality. So there are things we are reluctant to do, and things we are afraid to ask for, only to find out, as Abraham did, that people have been counting on us to do these things all along.

What is the image of the American Jew in the eyes of our non-Jewish neighbors? We know what the anti-Semites think of us, and we know what the Christian missionaries think of us. But the average American is neither a missionary nor an anti-Semite. What does he or she think of us? I suspect Americans see us as a lot stronger, a lot more secure and less vulnerable than we see ourselves, and in some cases, they see us much as Abraham's Canaanite neighbors saw him, as *n'si Elohim atta b'tocheinu*, the embodiment of God's presence in their midst.

A valuable resource in determining that would be the ten thousand people every year who become Jewish by choice. Born gentile, they convert to Judaism, sometimes to marry into a Jewish family, sometimes to complete a personal spiritual pilgrimage of their own, and occasionally to do both at once. I meet a new candidate for the conversion process about once a month, and in the course of the intake interview, I ask what he or she already knows about Jews and Judaism. Granted, these candidates may not be typical American Christians. There are very few anti-Semites or fundamentalists among them. Some of them probably had a more favorable than average opinion of Judaism even before they became romantically involved with someone Jewish. But they do represent a cross section of gentile America in their religious, educational, and even geographic background, so what they tell me, I think, is significant. And what is even more amazing, they all tell me the same thing, and I think that makes their testimony even more valuable.

The first thing that strikes them about Judaism is its moral seriousness. We are a people who cares, a people who speak out in the name of social and economic justice. We care about this world. Where others narrow their focus to their own salvation, leaving a sinful world behind, or where others balance the unfairness of this world with the promise of a perfect life in the hereafter, Jews are so outraged at this world's unfairness that we wear ourselves out to do something about it, to help the poor, the starving, the oppressed. Barely over 2 percent of the American population (which nobody believes, because we are so conspicuous), we are overrepresented in almost all efforts to make this world more nearly resemble the Kingdom of God, the decent society God summoned us to build. Moral seriousness— we are among the very few American groups willing to put the well-being of all America ahead of their own self-interest. As Milton Himmelfarb put it after a recent election, Jews are still the only people who earn like Episcopalians and vote like Puerto Ricans. Consistently, we don't vote for the Jewish candidate, or even the most pro-Israel candidate (although we will vote against the candidate who seems unreliable on Israel). Consistently, we vote for the candidate most likely to make ours a more decent and more compassionate society.

We are a charitable people, and America knows it and counts on us for it. Foolish people still make jokes about the Jewish craving for money, but people who know what is going on in American life know that no university and no museum, no medical research and no civil rights organization can balance its budget without Jewish support. Though just 2 percent of the population, we make America a more generous, more compassionate society by our generosity.

The other big thing these non-Jews considering becoming Jewish always tell me about is the warmth and closeness of the Jewish family. We've grown up with it so much that we take it for granted. We assume all families hug and kiss and fight and argue over trivialities. We assume all parents contemplate taking out an ad in the *Globe* when their child brings home a straight-A report card. Philip Roth has even enlightened us on how smothering and destructive that kind of love is. But when you've lived outside and seen it from the outside, you envy it. You know how rare and life-enhancing that kind of warmth is in a cold world.

In an America where the family is falling apart, people are looking to us to teach them how to be a family. In an America where everybody is increasingly looking out for himself, people see the Jewish community as a rare and glowing instance of people still feeling they have obligations for one another. They know what we do for Israel, they know what we do for Soviet Jewry, and if from time to time they talk about it in accents of resentment, I think a lot of it is envy. They wish they had somebody who belonged to them that way. *Fiddler on the Roof* wasn't a long-running hit solely because of synagogue theater parties. All of America responded to something authentic in Tevya's family that they found missing in their own.

The key word, I think, is "authentic." People see the Jewish community as an authentic community, where people really care about one another and about the world they live in. They see the Jewish family as a real family, deeply entangled with one another's lives, not an accidental concatenation of semi-independent individuals sharing the same address. And they understand how much they need that kind of authenticity.

The problem is, those qualities are true of Judaism. I'm not sure they are true of American Jews. I'm not sure our families are still that different from other families. I wonder if we haven't lost the art of being generous, of giving to the needy first and then seeing if there is enough left for a winter vacation instead of the other way around.

And the reason for the change is that we don't know our own strength. The first generation of Jews that moved out to the suburbs was so concerned about being accepted, about fitting in. We were convinced that in order for our new neighbors to like us, we had to persuade them that we were just like them. So we set out to abandon everything that made us us. One sarcastic comment from a Little League coach and we decided our child didn't really have to go to Junior Congregation. One impatient remark by a ballet teacher was enough to convince us that regular attendance at religious school wasn't all that much of a priority. One funny look from a stranger at a barbecue, and we decided that keeping kosher was a relic from another age. Like Abraham, we saw ourselves as ger and toshav, not sure if we really belonged out here or if we were still waiting on approval. And in the process, we missed out on an important truth. Our new neighbors didn't want imitation gentiles. Why should they when they could find so many real ones so easily? Our strength had always been that we were a people who took God's word seriously, no matter what others said about us, but suddenly we could only see our weakness and forget our strength. We couldn't quite believe that America would really let us be ourselves, and when like Abraham's neighbors, they not only told us they would, but told us they needed us to do that, we were more than a little bit astonished.

Let me give you an example. Not that long ago, an important figure in American Jewish history died: Hank Greenberg, the Hall of Fame first baseman for the Detroit Tigers in the 1930s and 1940s. He was the first Jewish superstar athlete. The obituary notices last month spoke of the year he hit fifty-eight home runs, of his record for runs batted in, of his being the first ballplayer to earn $100,000 a year. But none of the ones I read included my favorite Hank Greenberg story. One year when the High Holy Days came early and the pennant race ran late, Greenberg faced the dilemma of playing or not playing a key game on Yom Kippur. Greenberg, needless to say, was not a very observant Jew. He felt an obligation to his teammates to play, but at the same time he felt an obligation to himself, to his own authenticity, to take the day off. Most Jews encouraged him to play, because they were afraid the non-Jewish world would resent it if the team lost because he wasn't there, and in their understanding of Judaism there was nothing more important than not offending the non-Jewish world. Ultimately he decided not to play. He went to shul instead and to everyone's surprise, all of Detroit and all of American applauded his decision.

The Hearst newspaper in Detroit, ordinarily no friend of the Jews, put his picture on the front page with the headline, "L'Shana Tova". The lesson, it seems to me, was this: America cheers for winners but America respects people of integrity more. There is always a winner. Every year, somebody wins, sometimes by talent, sometimes by cheating, sometimes by good luck. There are lots of success stories, accounts of people making it to the top by not caring about anything except making it to the top. But there are all too few stories about people who cared more about being true to themselves than they did about winning. We win a place in America's heart by daring to be true to our authentic selves.

Where is America today? America is uncomfortable with the kind of society it is becoming. America is embarrassed by its music and its movies, by its poverty and its urban crime. American is desperately looking for some sort of moral guidance. That is why people turn to the mindless bigotry of Jimmy Swaggart and the arrogance of Pat Robertson. That is why people with college degrees are turning to the fundamentalist churches and the Lubavitcher *shtiblekh*. They are looking for moral seriousness, for spiritual authenticity. America needs people to show it how to be a decent, compassionate society again. America wants to be good and doesn't know how. And we let America down when we are afraid to be the people are supposed to be.

We don't know our own strength. We don't realize how much people are depending on us to be authentic Jews, to change the air and show the way. They are depending on us to show them what a family looks like, what a community looks like, what generosity looks like. But when they look to us, they see us trying to look like them. And that's what they resent. That's when they feel betrayed and let down.

A generation ago, two generations ago, out of our love for this country which welcomed us and promised us freedom, we thought that the nicest thing we could do for America in return was to shed our differences in the melting pot and become like everybody else. We would change our names, we would change our habits. We would learn to drink and cheat and run around, just like real Americans. And we were so flattered when somebody said to us, "You don't look Jewish." We did that, not because we loved Judaism less; we felt very loyal to Judaism. But we did it because we loved America more, and we thought that was what America wanted. We meant well, but we were wrong. America already had enough people who were like everybody else.

Today, out of our love for this country which has treated us so well, we understand that the nicest thing we can do for America is to be good Jews, to be our authentic selves. The American soul is not enriched by imitation. It is enriched by people of integrity and moral seriousness. It respects authentic people, people who know who they are and bear it proudly. More than respect, it envies them. If we would be bold enough to lay claim to the strength that is ours, strength we did not know we had, the strength that comes from being yourself and not feeling you have to wear a borrowed mask, then we would hear our neighbors say with gratitude and admiration, as Abraham heard his neighbors say, "*N'si Elohim atta b'tocheynu*, You are the people who bring God down to earth in our midst. You are the people for whom we lift the lamp beside the golden door."

PAIN AND PRIDE

I was born and grew up in Brooklyn, in the neighborhood known as Crown Heights, a neighborhood that is now the flashpoint for the confrontation between blacks and Hassidic Jews, followers of the Lubavitcher Rebbe. This is the neighborhood where the riots and the murder of a yeshiva student took place some years ago. And for someone like me who still cherishes memories of Montgomery Street and Eastern Parkway, for someone like me who was active in the civil rights movement of the 1960s, who met and marched and rallied with Martin Luther King, it is painful to see the angry confrontation between Jews and blacks in the streets where I grew up, went to synagogue, and absorbed the values of Judaism.

But what makes it doubly painful is not only argument, but the terms in which the argument is being conducted. Both sides, Jew and black alike, are trying to score debaters' points by arguing over which side has suffered more. Jews are saying, "Granted, slavery was terrible. Granted, people were whipped, humiliated; families were separated. But how can you compare it to Auschwitz? There were no gas chambers on the plantations. There were no sadistic scientific experiments, babies being tortured in the presence of their mothers. There were no killing squads making hundreds of people dig their own graves and then shooting them. How can you compare slavery at its worst with that?" and black people are answering, "Don't talk to us about how you can sympathize with us because you've suffered too. The Holocaust lasted six years; slavery lasted six generations. And how can you compare discrimination in white-collar employment and country club membership to what black men and women have to go through every day of their lives at the hands of the police?" Jews complain about being mugged by black drug addicts, and black people complain about being robbed by Jewish storekeepers and employers.

It's all so sad and it's all so futile, part of what Robert Hughes calls the "culture of complaint," the assumption that an individual or group has a claim on other people's sympathy because they have suffered, and the more you have suffered, the more urgent and legitimate your claim.

It's sad and it's futile in part because both sides are right and both are wrong. Slavery *was* a two-century-long violation of human dignity from which black people have still not entirely recovered. And the Holocaust *was* an indescribably atrocity which continues to cast a shadow over Jewish-Christian relations.

But this culture of complaint, this competition to gain a moral advantage by claiming you have suffered more, is wrong for a whole lot of reasons. First of all, it doesn't work. Telling people they owe you something because you have suffered occasionally evokes sympathy, but more often evokes a sense of resentment, especially if it's phrased as a demand rather than a plea. Moreover, at least as far as Jewish history is concerned, it's historically inaccurate. No matter what you remember being taught in Hebrew school, no matter what your grandmother told you about how hard it is to be a Jew, the fact of the matter is, Jewish history is not primarily an account of persecution and suffering. It is primarily a story of great historical spiritual achievement.

Last spring, I visited the Holocaust Memorial Museum in Washington, D.C. If you haven't been there, let me tell you, it is a stunning achievement. The building is an architectural masterpiece. It manages to be soaring and elegant and spacious, and at the same time feel heavy and confining. The displays are expertly done. But as I was going through the museum and being deeply moved by it, there was another voice inside my head offering a counterargument, saying, "If we have the attention of the American public for one hour, is this really the message we want to give them? The Jew as victim? Is this what we want these Girl Scouts from Georgia and these tourists from Kansas and these black teenagers form the District of Columbia to learn about the Jews, how much we've suffered?" On the one hand, we have the obligation to tell the story, because there are so many people who doubt it, who don't want to believe it, and because the last wish of so many of the victims was that they not be forgotten, that their story be told to the world. But on the other hand, there are too many Christians and too many Jews who find it convenient: Christians, as a summary of their belief that Jews are being eternally punished for having rejected Jesus; and Jews, because it enables them to avoid taking the real message of Judaism seriously.

But most of Jewish history is not about persecution and martyrdom. The communities that Hitler destroyed were great, creative communities. You're talking about the piety and scholarship of Eastern Europe. You're talking about the German-speaking Jewish communities of Europe that gave the world Einstein and Freud and Kafka and Mahler. If the only thing the world comes to know about these communities is that a man named Hitler came along and killed them, that's like writing a book about American history that tells you nothing about Abraham Lincoln except that he was assassinated. Where is the museum about what Jews have done for the world, to stand alongside the museum about what the world has done to the Jews?

The third thing that is wrong with that emphasis on victimhood is that it's educationally and psychologically dysfunctional. Tell a child that "the whole world is against us" and he's likely to wonder if maybe the whole world isn't right. It's hard for a young person to stand up to the opinion of the whole world. He may end up, especially if he is insecure to being with, siding with the bullies instead of the victims. It seems safer. So you get black children who want to play with blond Barbie dolls, and black adults who gain status in the black community by being relatively light-skinned. You get Jews who tell jokes that perpetuate anti-Semitic stereotypes and who still think it is a compliment to be told "You don't look Jewish." And perhaps worst of all, you find these members of minority groups looking for someone to hate so that they can be in the majority for a change, the victimizer rather than the one victim.

More than that, there is a danger that this rooting of one's identity in a sense of victimization, this emphasis on Jewish suffering or black suffering or the oppression of women, this constant harping on "look what the world has done to us" will breed a sense of passivity. It frees you from responsibility. Your situation is now somebody else's fault, and there is nothing you can do or need to do about it. But if the comfort level of Jews in this country is a function of anti-Semitism, how many anti-Semites there are and how hard they work at it, if anti-Semitism is the only barrier to assimilating and the only real reason for remaining Jewish, if the only reason we can give our children not to intermarry is that deep down gentiles really dislike us, then our enemies will have the power to decide how Jewish we and our children will be.

Now, if this process of rooting so much of your identity in a sense of victimhood is factually wrong and psychologically crippling, why are so many people doing it? Partly there is something perversely satisfying about seeing yourself as a victim. It lets you feel morally superior. It lets you excuse yourself for moments of callousness or bigotry by letting you say, "After what they've done to us, I don't owe them anything."

But I think a large part of it is the widespread assumption that if you do it right, you can go through your whole life without ever being hurt, and if you should ever feel pain, you are entitled to find out whose fault it was and be compensated.

Yet what worries me about that attitude is that if you start out thinking "life should never hurt," the next step is liable to be "I don't want to be Jewish, because to be a Jew is to be the one who gets hurt."

Example: in the past year, I've read no fewer than four articles in Jewish publications on the subject I had almost never seen written about before, the notion that it is cruel and barbaric to subject a one-week-old Jewish baby boy to a *bris*, a ritual circumcision. Behind the argument is the thoroughly unrealistic attitude of so many young parents that "I don't want any child of mine to find out that life is painful." Now, aside from the fact that there is no reason to believe that circumcision at that age is particularly painful, aside from the fact that this is a ritual that has been performed tens of millions of times with no evidence that Jewish men are traumatized by it, what about the idea that part of one's Jewish identity, part of what it means to be a Jew, is the recognition that if you do it right, life *will* be painful because you will be sensitive to all the things that go wrong in the world. This not the Jew as victim; it's the Jew as person who cares deeply about injustice, whether done to him or to someone else. I think one of his classical statements of what it means to be Jewish is in the movie *Annie Hall*, where the Woody Allen character wants to go to see a five-hour movie about the Holocaust while his non-Jewish girlfriend wants to go to a movie to be entertained.

If you don't teach your children that feeling pain is an indispensable part of being an honorable human being, where will they learn to remain in a relationship when the fun and novelty have worn off? Where will they learn to take care of *you* when you are old and needy—and caring for a sick, needy parent is not anyone's idea of fun—if you have taught them that they never have to do anything painful?

Friends of ours recently told us how their daughter nursed her best friend through a long, agonizing death from AIDS, and how they tried to discourage her in the beginning but now are proud of the fact that they raised a young woman who had the courage and loyalty to do that.

I think one of the great stories of this past year is the way the Jewish world has spoken out on behalf of the Bosnian Muslims while almost no one else has. Think about it: after what Muslim leaders have been saying about us and about Israel for forty years, we didn't respond by saying, "Big deal; we had it worse, now it's their turn." We saw pain where other people saw only politics. That's not the Jew as victim; it's the Jew as person who cares about victims.

Second example: the parents who come to the religious school office to complain that their children aren't enjoying religious school. "It's not fun." And the parents—maybe the same parents—who complain to the public schools that, because of all their other commitments and favorite television programs (which can be very educational), one hour of homework a night is the most their children can handle. No, it's probably *not* fun to sit in a classroom for several hours a day. Learning may be rewarding, it may be enriching, but there are a lot of things that are more fun. But life is more than a search for pleasure and avoidance of pain. That is the kind of life animals live. For human beings, life is a search for meaning and an avoidance of triviality. For the mature person, life is a matter of understanding that the path to fulfillment sometimes passes through the door marked pain.

Athletes understand that. They understand that they can't rely on natural ability. They have to subject themselves to strenuous conditioning drills to be the ballplayers they want to be. Musicians understand that. They know they have to spend hours on routine exercises before they can create beauty. People on diets understand that. They know that in order to look and feel the way they want to look and feel, they can't phrase the question in terms of "what would be the most fun to eat?" and college students have to learn that college is a place to acquire wisdom, a place to stretch their minds, not a place to have a blast for four years before facing the responsibilities of the real world.

I remember many years ago meeting with a young couple who were going to get married here at Temple Israel. I would be doing the wedding, and I wanted to get to know them and go over the ceremony with them. Everything was going smoothly enough until at one point the young man, the prospective bridegroom, said, "Rabbi Kushner, would you be willing to make one small change in the Jewish wedding ceremony Instead of pronouncing us husband and wife until death do us part, would you pronounce us husband and wife for as long as our love lasts? We've talked about this, and we've agreed that if we ever get to the point where we no longer love each other, it's not morally right for us to be stuck with each other."

I said to him, "No, I'm not going to make that change. I appreciate the distaste for hypocrisy which leads you to make that request. But what I'm hearing behind your words is that you're afraid to commit yourself totally to the marriage for fear it will hurt too much if you give yourself totally to it and it doesn't work out. Maybe you saw your parents' marriage when you were growing up and said, 'I don't want to end up like that.' Maybe you had a good friend who trusted someone and was hurt by that person, or maybe you yourself were hurt by someone in that way, and you responded by saying 'I'll never let anyone get that close to be able to hurt me like that again.' But if you don't invest yourself totally in this marriage because you don't want to run the risk of being hurt, if your attitude to pain is 'somebody did me wrong' rather than 'this is part of the process of being alive and caring,' then you're guaranteeing that it won't work because you won't care enough to make it work."

In a similar way, there is a cynicism about politics, about public service, because we've been hurt and disappointed so often by public officials we trusted. A generation that gave its heart to John Kennedy had its heart broken, first when he was killed and then again when we learned details of his private life. And because of that experience, we're reluctant to give our hearts away again. We suspect the worst of everyone in public life. And how you calculate the harm done to the American civic structure by a mind-set that says of everyone running for public office "you can't trust them, they're all a bunch of phonies"?

We play it safe. We're careful not to give our hearts away without a guarantee that we won't be disappointed this time. We go around wearing a suit of armor so that nobody can hurt us. And as a result, we feel no pain, but we feel no joy, no hope. We don't feel anything. Our lives are numb, anesthetized.

I think that explains in part why so many Christians are leaving the conventional main-line churches for fundamentalist, evangelical gatherings where the emotional temperature is higher. And it explains the secret, grudging envy many of us feel for the Hassidim. We can't accept their ideas about the world, and we're not about to adopt their lifestyle, but we wish we could believe what we believe as fervently as they believe what they believe. We wish we were brave enough to really believe in *something*, to root our lives in something that would permit us to take off the armor and dare to feel again.

Being a serious Jew is not a matter of setting yourself up to suffer, to be a victim. Maybe a hundred years ago in Russia that was the case, maybe fifty years ago in Germany. But even then, I suspect, the years of holiness outweighed the weeks and months of anguish. To be a serious Jew does not put you in line to suffer, but it does expose you to pain—the pain of being alive, the pain of making difficult moral choices, the pain of knowing how far short the world has fallen of what God wants it to be. But it is only by feeling that pain that we know we are alive. You can cut your hair or your fingernails and not feel it because those are dead cells. But cut into living flesh and it hurts precisely because it is alive.

To hide from pain is to hide from life for fear that life might hurt. To shield our children from knowing that life is sometimes painful is to anesthetize them against the whole range of feeling that go with being alive. The real pain that goes with being Jewish is not the pain of the victims, the pain that robs life of its meaning. It is more like the pain of a woman in labor, that pain that gives birth to new life.

When Rachel, the wife of Jacob in the Bible, gives birth to a son after years of childlessness, she names him Joseph, which means "increase, add," saying as she does so *"Yosef li Adonai ben acher,* May God increase my family and give me more children." She has just gone through the pain of childbirth, and her first prayer is that she undergo that pain again because it is the kind of pain that enhances life. In the words of Kahlil Gibran, "The deeper that sorrow carves into your being, the more joy you can contain." A colleague of mine, a rabbi in a nearby community, when he learned that he had cancer, responded not by asking, "Why me?" but by asking, "What can I learn from this? How can I grow as a result? This is a once-in-a-lifetime experience and I don't want to waste it on self-pity."

The pain a Jew feels when he identifies with the oppressed, the pain a Jew feels when he stands up for what is right but unpopular, the pain of having to give up something you want because it conflicts with something you believe in—that is not the pain of being a victim. That is the pain that increases life. When we pray this morning for a year of life, we are not asking for a year free from all pain. That would be a year of numbness, a year spent under anesthesia, a year of not being truly alive. We ask instead for the ability to accept the pain that is an inevitable part of being alive, of being human, of being Jewish. We pray that, if we must feel pain during the coming year—and if we are to be human, then we will feel it—let it be growing pain, the pain of shedding bad habits that confine us and growing into new areas of life. Let it be not the pain of the victim, but the pain of the person who cares, the person who dares to love, to share, to feel the anguish of another soul. Remember us unto life, O Lord, and if we must feel pain, let it be the pain that reminds us that we are most authentically Jewish and most truly alive.

On Being
a Conservative Jew

Your homework assignment is to complete the following sentence: "My being Jewish is important to me and to others because …" You don't have to finish it today. You don't have to hand it in to me to be graded. But, at some point in your life—and maybe more than once—you have to figure out what your answer to that sentence would be. Neatness and spelling do not count, but you have to do your own work. You can't use somebody else's answer.

In the same way that one of the life-tasks of growing up is figuring out what it means to be a man or a woman, what it means to your life to be a husband or a wife, to be a parent—you can't make a decision about your life pretending that your children aren't there or that your parents don't exist—in that same way, the process of becoming a mature adult includes figure out how your life is different, how other people's lives are different, because you're Jewish.

In all the years that I have served this congregation, giving a sermon every Sabbath and every holiday for fourteen years, I don't think I've spoken more than once on what it means to be a Conservative Jew. That one time was when we first began to call women to the Torah, and I wanted to set that change in the context of our attitude toward Jewish Law. The rest of the time, I was content to talk about Judaism, rather than Conservative Judaism, because most of the time I think in those terms. I would talk about what it meant to be a human being in a very confusing and unreliable world, because then I knew I was answering *your* questions, not somebody else's questions. But today, for the second time in fourteen years, I want to talk about what it means to be a Conservative Jew, because I think a lot of us understand it in superficial terms (we think it means belonging to a synagogue where the service is in Hebrew and the men wear yarmulkes, or we think it means feeling guilty every time you go to a Chinese restaurant), and because last spring, the chancellor of the Jewish Theological Seminary challenged the rabbis and synagogue leaders of the Conservative movement to develop a Conservative lifestyle.

He said that if somebody describes himself as orthodox, you know immediately not only what he believes, but how he lives, how he dresses, what he eats, how he spends his time. The early pioneers in Israel, the *halut-zim*, had a distinctive lifestyle. Their ideology translate itself into a distinctive way of living, working, dressing Jewish socialists had a lifestyle—the newspapers they read, the things they talked about, the activities that consumed their time. What, he asked, is the lifestyle of an American Conservative Jew? It's not at all a clear picture.

And secondly, Chancellor Cohen said to us, each of these groups—the orthodox, the Zionist, the socialist—had an eschatology. That's a big theological word that means they had a vision of the future. They knew how they wanted the world to be different, and they believed that, by living the way they did, they were helping to make the world different in that way. That belief gave them the energy, the motivation to *live* by their commitments even when it wasn't convenient. I think we all know that feeling. The man who believes that what he does at work is really important and matters to people will manage to get to work even when it's snowing out and even when he doesn't feel well. The man who feels' he's just going through the motions is a lot more likely to decide that it's "impossible" for him to come in today. And in the area of religious observance, the person who relegates it to the periphery of his life, who believes it's a nice thing, a quaint old custom but not something that really matters, will be a lot quicker to decide that something is "impossible" when what he really means is "inconvenient" or "too expensive."

What I want to do is address myself to two questions: What is the lifestyle of a Conservative Jew? And what is the eschatology, the vision of the future, of the Conservative Jew? I'm not going to talk about yarmulkes, or how many sets of dishes you have. I think those are secondary details. They have their place, but this isn't the place for them. But I am going to suggest three things that I think every Conservative Jew ought to do, and I invite you to measure your own life, your own home, against this checklist.

First, I think that being a Conservative Jew involves a serious, open-minded confrontation with Jewish tradition, a willingness to learn more than you now know and to do more than you now do. It begins with a reluctance to dismiss any category of Jewish traditions out of hand. It has to start with the assumption that, if something has been an important part of Jewish life for a long time, there must be something to it. It's got to be more than primitive pseudoscience or superstition. It seems to me that it requires an unacceptable level of chutzpah to say, "Maimonides was foolish, Rabbi Akiba was foolish, the Gaon of Vilna was foolish, but me—I'm smart. I understand these things better than they did."

You know the story about the woman who comes to the rabbi and says, "Rabbi, you've got to help me do something about my son. I think he's losing his mind. Every morning, he winds these black leather straps around his arm and mumbles something in Hebrew. And when I bring food home from the market, he won't eat it until he's read over the list of ingredients. Rabbi, could you talk to him and straighten him out?" The rabbi says, "Madam, you're putting me in a very awkward position. You know, I also daven in the morning with tefillin, and I also eat only kosher food." And the woman answers, "Oh, I know that, Rabbi, but you have to do it for a living. My son means it."

If you think that's funny, you should hear some of the conversations I regularly have with people who confidently inform me that keeping kosher may have made some sense back when there were no refrigerators to keep the pork chops from spoiling, and laws about adultery made sense in a society where the wife was seen as the husband's property, but isn't that all really obsolete today? And when I tell them that I think I understand the religious impulses of the human spirit at least as well as they do, and I don't find either kashrut or martial fidelity obsolete, they smile and answer like the woman in the story: "Of course, Rabbi, you have to say that. That's your job. But just between us, off the record, don't you agree they're really silly?"

Before we even talk about levels of *observance*, it seems to me that we owe the Jewish tradition a certain level of *humility*, a hesitation to write something off before we've really understood it. My hero in this is Franz Rosenzweig, the German-Jewish philosopher who was a friend and contemporary of Martin Buber. Rosenzweig grew up in a nonobservant home, discovered serious Judaism as an adult, and wrote about Jewish observance with the enthusiasm of someone who had stumbled on a great and valuable buried treasure.

One evening, at one of his lectures, someone asked Rosenzweig if, with all his eloquent words about nearness to God, he put on tefillin and prayed every morning. Rosenzweig didn't know how to answer. He didn't pray every day, so obviously he couldn't lie and say Yes. But he didn't want to say No, to sound as if he had dismissed a basic ingredient of Jewish life as unimportant to him.

So he answered, "Not Yet."

"Not Yet" is a brilliant answer. It implies, "I don't do it, not because it's foolish or outmoded, but because I haven't gotten to the point where that particular observance speaks to me. But I can imagine myself someday starting to do it," as several families in this congregation have made their homes kosher in the past few years as a logical extension of their growth as Jews, as people have formed the habit of regular congregational worship, of being more responsive to charity than they were a few years ago, because even when they were nonobservant, they kept an open mind on the subject.

It reminds me of a humanities course I had in college, where the midyear exam consisted of two questions. First the professor asked us, "Of all the books we have read so far this year, which one did you appreciate least?" He gave us fifteen minutes to write our answers, then announced the second question, "To what limitation in yourself do you attribute this inability to appreciate a classic?"

"Not Yet." There is a spiritual difference between the Jew who works on the Sabbath and the Jew who stays home and spends part of the day in synagogue. I think we can all appreciate that. But there is also a spiritual difference between the Jew who goes to work—or to the store or the beauty parlor or mows his lawn on Saturday because the Sabbath means nothing to him or her, because the idea of doing things differently today because it's Shabbat is irrelevant, out of left field—and the Jew who works on Saturday because his job, his line of work requires it but he knows he's missing out on something, he knows he has had to make a choice, or the Jew who knows that there is such a thing as Shabbat but he hasn't yet come to the point where it speaks to him in a commanding voice. There is, it seems to me, a spiritual difference between the person who goes to the beach or drives to visit relatives on Saturday because he has the day off, and the person who does the same things as a form of Oneg Shabbat, an effort to fill the Sabbath day with a certain kind of pleasure.

One of the assumptions of the High Holy Day season is that people are capable of changing, of growing, of outgrowing old habits and becoming different. When the modern Jew confronts the ancient Jewish tradition, we can hope that he will say Yes to much of it, but we can demand that at the very least, he say Not Yet.

That sense of humility that says, "We need to learn more and to grow more before we dare to pass final judgment on any detail of Jewish tradition" is the first ingredient of a Conservative Jewish lifestyle. The second and third are what I would call Jewish space and Jewish time. Jewish space means that there ought to be a tangible, physical Jewish presence in your home. At the very least, a mezuzah on the doorpost; Shabbat candlesticks; Jewish books on your shelf, and not just Philip Roth and Belva Plain, but the beginnings of a basic Jewish library. I saw a bulletin board outside a church one day that read, "If you were arrested for being a Christian, would there be enough evidence to convict?" We can ask, "If someone investigated where we lived and how we lived, how long would it take him to find out that we were Jewish?"

Jewish time means that you regularly do something different because you're Jewish—going to services or praying at home, reading a Jewish book or gathering the family on Friday night to bless the candles and welcome the Sabbath. Jewish time can mean making the Sabbath day different from the weekday in some consciously and recognizably Jewish fashion. I knew two young men, one a medical student and one a college football player, whose schedules made Saturday the busiest day of their week. They would take paperback books of Jewish thought along and find fifteen minutes to read them, just to remember that, although they were busy, it was Shabbat. Jewish time can be volunteer work at the hospital or with the League of Women Voters, if you are doing that as part of the mitzvah of being of service to others, and not just because you're a middle-class suburban housewife whose children are grown up.

Allocating time is the way we show what we really care about, because the demands on our time are so many. And allocating time is the way we declare who we are, because we are what we do. We define ourselves not by what we believe, not by what we feel, not by what we're in favor of, but by what we do.

And that brings us to the last ingredient, the eschatology, the vision of how the world will be different if we take our Jewishness seriously. When I was young, I would read the story of Abraham on Rosh HaShanah, and I would respond to Abraham the young man, who broke the idols his father worshipped and set out to find his own way. I'm older now, and now when I read the story of Abraham every Rosh HaShanah, I find myself responding to Abraham the parent, who is desperately concerned that his children follow in his path. "What good is everything I've accomplished," he says to God, "if I don't have a child who will follow me?" I can visualize Abraham saying to Isaac, "When I was your age, I thought the most important thing in the world was to pass judgment on what my father believed, and to find things out for myself. Now I understand the most important thing in the world is to come to terms with who I am, including being his child and being your father, and to figure out what my life really means."

But how do you get children to follow your path? You can't make them do it for your sake, out of guilt or out of loyalty. You can't even make them do it for their own sake, by telling them they'll be happier. But I think young people will do it for the world's sake, as a way of making the world better. Why do bright Jewish children join the Moonies or Hare Krishna? One such child was interviewed recently and said, "All my parents ever wanted from me was to get into college, get a good job, and make money. Reverend Moon wants me to help him save the world." That's what we're competing for with young people's souls.

Do you know the story of the lion-tamer at the circus? One day, the lion-tamer got sick, so he called in one of the circus handymen and said to him, "I'm not feeling well, I can't go on tonight. You'll have to fill in for me in the lion-taming act. It's really simple; I'll tell you how to do it. Take a chain in one hand and a whip in the other, and let the lion know that you're not afraid of him." The handyman looked at him and said, "I don't think I could ever be that deceitful."

If I didn't think that the world needed observant Jews, living exemplars of Jewish tradition from a non-Orthodox, non-fundamentalist point of view, I couldn't stand up here and ask you to change your lifestyle to be more observant. If I thought it was just a matter of going through the motions to keep some quaint old customs from dying out, there would be no conviction to my urging it. Like the substitute lion-tamer, I couldn't be that deceitful. And if *you* don't believe that the world needs committed Jews, then you won't be able to fool your children either. Abraham, who rebelled against his father's values, taught his son to follow *his* values, not because he was a better parent or a more eloquent speaker, but because when he spoke, you knew he meant it. You felt the conviction. He believed the world depended on his son's following God's ways.

What is it the world needs? I can't say to you that the world needs people who won't eat lobster. That's trivial. But I do think the world desperately needs people who know how to control their instincts, their appetites of all sorts, people who can have something tempting within their reach and say No to it. I think the world needs that more than it needs anything else I can think of.

I think the world desperately needs the examples of modern, educated people taking issues of God and faith and self-control seriously, as an alternative to unthinking, unenlightened fundamentalism on the one hand and a super sophisticated sense of "anything goes" on the other.

I can't credibly tell you that the world will be redeemed if more Jews came to shul and read psalms and hear my sermons. But I can see the world being redeemed by the example of people who say, "I have to earn a living, but at least one day a week, there will be some things more important to me than getting and spending money. My family is one of them. My peace of mind is one of them. My soul is one of them."

I believe that a few people, by their example, can change a community. I've seen it happen. And a few communities can change a whole society. Four percent of Israelis live on kibbutzim, but the kibbutzim have set the moral tone for much of Israel. They are a disproportionate part of Israel's soul, even as the heart and brain take up a relatively small part of the human body compared to some other organs, but they determine what that body is all about. 3 percent of Americans are Jewish. But we have managed to set the tone for the nation's literature, movies, education, philanthropy, and much of its retail business. If we would work as hard at the challenge of religion as we have worked at those things, we could have the same effect. We could do more than gratify our grandparents and impress our children by taking our Jewishness seriously. Like Abraham, we could make a pagan world into a world fit for God.

POWER AND GOODNESS

It all began with Abraham, and that is why, on Rosh HaShanah, we turn back in our Torah readings to the story of Abraham, and read it again.

It all began with Abraham; and I confess that I would be more comfortable with that statement if I knew more specifically what that "it" referred to. Abraham is the pioneer of the Jewish faith, the first person to have a new concept of God and a new understanding of our relationship to Him. But because the Torah is not a book of theology, it never tells us just what Abraham's new idea about God was.

When my book about suffering came out, a colleague of mine, a Conservative rabbi of somewhat more traditional leanings, wrote a negative review of it in which he said that, by denying that God was all-powerful, by denying that He controlled everything that happened in the world, I was reading myself out of traditional Jewish theology. He said he thought I was a nice person and he was sorry for all the personal sorrow my family had gone through, but he could not understand how I as a rabbi could deny that God was all-powerful. Jewish theology, he said, goes back to Abraham and the claim of monotheism that God *is* all-powerful because there are no other gods.

I wrote back to him after I read the review, thanking him for all of his kind words and thanking him too for clarifying so well what the issue between us was. I said to him, "You see the basic idea of Abraham's monotheism as being that God is all-powerful. I see the basic idea of Abraham's monotheism as being that God demands morality, that He stands for what is morally right. Where there are many gods, there cannot be one morality. There can only be a power struggle; what is right in the eyes of one god is unacceptable to others. You remember all those scenes in Homer's *Iliad*, where the gods take sides and get into quarrels. But when there is only one God, He can proclaim what is right and what is good."

Is God a symbol of Power or is He a symbol of Goodness? That is not an abstract question to be discussed in college seminars. It is a very down-to-earth question, perhaps the most important moral question on anybody's agenda today. There is a struggle going on in Israel today for the soul of the Jewish state. This is a very difficult and dangerous hour for Israel, and we who love Israel owe it our support and our trust, perhaps more now than ever before. We show our love not by standing at a distance and judging, but by trying to feel our way into the situation there and taking some of their pain arid their perplexity onto ourselves. And one of the ways we help Israel is by' understanding just what the crisis is about. It is not simply about borders or about inflation arid the economy. If you peel off enough layers of rhetoric and get to the heart of the discussion, the argument is about whether God stands for Power or whether He stands for Goodness.

Something very strange and very disturbing has happened in Israel, in the Orthodox religious circles of Israel, in the last few years. There has emerged among the Israeli Orthodox a cult of toughness, a worship of power. It is among the most religious in Israel that you find the hard-line nationalists, the people who move not just into vacant lands on the West Bank, Judea and Samaria, but into the heart of Arab cities and neighborhoods with an attitude of "we belong here and you don't because God gave this land to us."

Two things happened this summer that caused me to worry about the Jewish soul of Israel. The first was the arrest of twenty-seven young men, all of them from yeshivot and observant backgrounds, for involvement in Jewish terrorist operations. They are accused of planting bombs in Arab cars and buses, and some of them of conspiring to blow up the Dome of the Rock, the golden-domed mosque in Jerusalem, in order to bring on the final showdown between Jews and Muslims. That was the first thing, a Jewish terrorist underground different from the one which operated against the British because this was done in violation of the laws of a Jewish government, a highly nationalistic, highly religiously committed government.

The second incident that shook me up and caused me very grave concern was an advertisement placed in the Israeli press by thirty-eight American Orthodox rabbis defending and justifying what those terrorists had been doing, including the danger to innocent people and the loss of any moral right to condemn Arab violence. I confess that I read that ad and could not recognize what they were saying as anything I knew as Judaism. Where is Judaism's regard for the sanctity of life? Where is our traditional concept of justice, of discriminating between the innocent and the guilty? The God they believed in was a God who could say, "The earth is mine and all the people in it; I can do whatever I want with them," not the God who was prepared to spare Sodom and Gomorrah if ten good people could be found in them, not the God who had to concede the rightness of Abraham's plea: "*Hashofet kol ha-aretz lo ya'aseh mishpat?* How can a God of Justice do something which is unjust?"

This is different form the case of the Orthodox Jew who is a slumlord or runs fraudulent nursing homes, different from the man who is scrupulously kosher in his diet but cheats people in his business. Those men are just hypocrites. The Jewish terrorists in Israel are not hypocrites. They are not embarrassed by what they were caught doing. They believe in the religious legitimacy of throwing grenades into schoolyards and planting dynamite in houses of worship. And they believe in it because they believe in a God of Might, a God of Power who has power over life and death, who can take from one and give to another as He chooses.

The first chief rabbi of Palestine before there was an Israel, Rabbi Avraham Yitzchak HaKohen Kook, was a mystic who had a vision of Israel being the source of a special light that it would shed on the world. He was a pacifist, a vegetarian who couldn't stand the thought of causing an animal pain to give him pleasure. He was a man overflowing with *ahavat Yisrael*, love for all Jews, religious and nonreligious, learned and ignorant, nice people and not-so-nice people. He loved them all. His son, Rabbi Zvi Yehuda Kook, translated that love for all Jews into a love for the land and for all the people who worked to build it. But somehow, the disciples of that father and son, students of the school that bears their name, heard the message about the land, but not the part about compassion and humility that went with it. They learned about God's special concern for Israel, but not about His special demands upon them. Love for every Jew somehow became translated into a lack of concern for anyone who was not a Jew. And in the process, Jewish faith became translated into something I don't recognize and cannot accept.

Again, it is not a question of boundaries. It is not a question of different views of Israel's security. It is the result of what happens when Jews come to worship power, when you define the essence of God as His Strength, His ability to control events, rather than His goodness or His moral vision. This summer, I read Barbara Tuchman's book *The March of Folly*, about the tendency of governments and human councils to act foolishly despite advice and evidence to the contrary. One of the forms that folly takes is the notion that, if you are powerful enough you can make things happen the way you want them to. You can write the script, you can pull all the strings. But the fact is, life never works out that way. No matter how powerful you are, life is too unpredictable, too full of imponderables. Ask Lyndon

Johnson, ask Richard Nixon how much power you need to have to make the script turn out exactly the way you want it to.

We can argue the pros and cons of the Israeli incursion into Lebanon several years ago. When it happened, I defended it on the radio, saying to a Christian Arab clergyman who criticized it, "If the Cubans had been shelling southern Florida so that schoolchildren in Miami had to live in underground shelters and people were afraid to go out in the street, how long would it have taken President Reagan to respond with force, and would you as an American citizen have criticized him for it?" He had no answer.

But in the long run, it turned out to be folly—maybe not immoral but foolish. And the reason it was foolish was that Israel thought it was strong enough to control events. They forgot the lesson of history that going to war can at best prevent something bad from happening; it can very rarely create something good. Religious people should have known better. They should have had the humility to know that none of us can shape the future. They should have remembered all the passages in the Midrash where even God can't control human events totally. They should have had more of that sense of dread at shedding blood that makes war a desperate last resort, not an attractive policy option. How could they have forgotten the teaching that King David was not permitted to build the Temple because he had been a warrior? Only his son Solomon, Shlomo the man of Shalom, would build it. They forgot because they had come to see God as a symbol of Power, to insist that He was omnipotent and to believe that as they become more powerful, more nearly omnipotent, they became more like God. To see God as representing Power is to deify Power, and when we believe In a God like that, the world becomes a meaner and more dangerous place.

This conflict between the face of God as representing Power and the face of God as representing Goodness, Righteousness, is not a new one. It has come up before in Jewish history, once almost at the beginning. Abraham's grandchildren could already no longer remember what Abraham's special idea had been. Do you remember who Abraham's grandchildren were? Jacob and Esau. Esau was a strong, physical man, a hunter, an intimidating person, a man of power. Jacob was a man of the spirit, soft and gentle, scaring no one, hurting no one, raising sheep instead of hunting deer. Each one claimed to be the heir of Abraham, each one wanted to be the third link in the chain of the patriarchs. Isaac their father had to choose between them, and he almost chose wrong. Perhaps because he had been a weak, vulnerable person all his life, perhaps because he had almost been murdered when he was a child and must have felt so powerless to prevent it, perhaps because all his life he had been intimidated by neighbors and enemies, Isaac was attracted to the brute strength of Esau. He wanted to give Esau the mantle of Abraham our father, and only the intervention of his wife, Rebecca (there was already a gender gap in those days), made sure that the blessing went instead to Jacob, and that it was from Jacob that the tribes of Israel would descend.

I see biblical history repeating itself in our beloved State of Israel. I see a people who have been defenseless and vulnerable for so long, a people whose children were murdered and there was nothing they could do to stop it, a people threatened and terrorized by conscienceless enemies and scorned by the international community— I see that people more attracted to the strength of Esau than to the spirit of Jacob. I see the voice of Jacob being drowned out by the hands of Esau. I see them worshipping the God who rained fire on Sodom and Gomorrah, not the God who promised Abraham that through his seed would all the nations of the world be blessed. And I want to stop and remind them that it was Jacob, not Esau, who carried on the message of Abraham, Jacob not Esau who wrestled with God and with his own conscience one dark night, and as a reward for that, Jacob was given the name Israel.

Is God a symbol of Power, of always being right and being able to control events, or is God a symbol of Goodness, of Righteousness, of a sometimes frustrating struggle to make in imperfect world even a little bit better? Is God all-powerful but not always good, or is He all-good, all-caring, but not always powerful? If God is what human beings at their best can resemble, if He is the Source toward which we climb and, the model after which we try to reshape ourselves, then what does it mean for us to bear the image of God? Does it mean to work at being more powerful, more controlling? Or does it mean to work at growing, caring, becoming a more sensitive person, because those are the qualities we associate with God? It is an urgent issue for Israel in its moral crisis, but it is an issue for every one of us in our daily lives as well. What kind of people do we want to be as husbands and wives, as mothers and fathers? If God is perfect, if God is the epitome of Power, then for us to be in the image of God, we would have to insist that we were always right. We would have to have everything done our way, just like God does. We could never admit a mistake, we could never compromise, because being less than perfect would mean a falling away from the image of an all-perfect, all-powerful God.

I get into a lot of debates with clergymen who can't accept the idea that God is not perfect, that what He makes happen is not always right, and what usually emerges is that they can't accept the idea that *they* are not perfect either, that they may be wrong. In three years, I have never had one Orthodox rabbi or one fundamentalist Christian minister say to me, "That's an interesting possibility; I'll have to think about that." Not once. It has always been "No, that's wrong, that's not the way it is." Now, that is not too bad in the case of a clergyman. After all, one of the things we pay clergy for is to believe a lot of dubious things on our behalf so that we don't have to believe them ourselves. But what happens when that attitude is held by a parent, or by a husband or wife: "I'm right and you're wrong and I'm not going to give in because I'll be less of a person if I do"? That's what happens when people deify Power instead of Goodness, when their inspiration, their image of God, is a totality of Power and perfection.

There are passages in the Bible, lots of them, where the image of God *is* an image of Power, where God speaks with a commanding voice: "Thou shalt! Thou shalt not!" But there are other passages where God reveals a different face, another voice, where He seems to want not so much obedience as relationship, not fear and respect but closeness and sharing. Sometimes God is a powerful King, but sometimes He is a vulnerable husband. One of the most beautiful instances of that comes in the Rosh HaShanah service. After we affirm God as King in Malchuyot, we come to Zichronot, the verses of remembering, and in Hebrew, the word "*zechor,*" to remember, as in Yizkor, often means an act of love. Remembering means holding on and not letting go. In one verse, God almost seems lonely. "*Zacharti lach hesed neurayich,* I remember the love of our younger days, the trust we had in each other then." God doesn't want to come across as so powerful that He overwhelms us, frightens us into compliance. He wants us close and sharing.

The Bible shows us God speaking in both voices, the voice of command and control, and the voice of love and sharing. No wonder we are confused as to what God is like, because the two, love and control, are incompatible. You can't love someone and also control him, make him do what you want. You can either love him or own him, but if you love him only for being compliant, for reflecting credit on you, for doing you will, that's not love. That's really just a roundabout way of loving yourself. That's why I believe God cherishes us more when we struggle to figure out what is right than He does when we look the rule up in a book and follow it out of fear. And that is why I believe a God of Power, a God who commands, is not the highest image of God. A God who invites us to grow, to become greater ourselves, rather than diminish ourselves to make Him seem bigger, is a much greater God. And a parent who summons a child to grow is much closer to the image of God than is a parent who thunders commands from the mountaintop and can't tell the difference between a good child and an obedient one.

A religion that worships a God of Power will teach people to serve God by obedience. Goodness means doing what is commanded. If it is successful, it will create a congregation of slaves, humble pious slaves who will do many good things and not too many bad ones, but slaves nonetheless. They may build cathedrals of stone and cathedrals of words that will dazzle the eye and mind, but the message of those cathedrals will be "God is great and we are nothing." And I'm sorry, I just can't believe God will be flattered by that message. If God is so great, how come the climax of His creation is nothing?

But if religion worships a God of Righteousness, then what we offer God is not our obedience but our integrity. We exalt God not by demonstrating how weak and dependent we are, but by showing how wondrous God's creatures can become. Like the father who is genuinely proud when his son grows to be taller than he is, like the husband who takes pride in his wife's achievements without resentment or jealousy, God is not diminished by our reaching for greatness. A God of Power needs to claim *all* power for Himself, but a God of Goodness is most righteous when He shares His goodness with us.

What was it that Abraham saw? What secret essence of God did he come to understand thirty-five hundred years ago? We can argue about it, but the answer is lost in the mists of time and we will never know. But I think that we can agree that in the State of Israel and here at Temple Israel, the shape of Jewish life and the shape of Jewish souls will be determined by whether we worship power or we worship goodness, not by what Abraham saw when he looked at God back then, but by what we see and do today when we come into His presence.

GOD LOVES US ANYWAY

One day about a year and a half ago, I was in Baltimore, Maryland, at the Johns Hopkins Medical Center. I had been invited to speak to the medical staff, the doctors and nurses, at noon, and to deliver a public lecture in the evening. After my talk to the staff, the hospital chaplain said to me, "There is one patient here who is very eager to meet you. He's read your book, he heard that you were coming, and asked if you could take the time to see him. Now, please understand, if you don't want to do this, you certainly don't have to. I'll just tell him you were too busy. His name is Rick Palomares, he's a thirty-two-year-old Episcopal clergyman who is dying of AIDS." I hesitated for a moment, then indicated that I'd be perfectly willing to see him. I went down there, feeling very noble and virtuous, feeling like I was the Jewish Mother Teresa, and I left fifteen minutes later feeling that I had gained much more from the encounter than I had given. It was a memorable experience.

I entered a room and saw a pale, thin man lying in bed, hooked up to tubes. I said, "How are you doing?" and he answered, "Not too good but I'm getting used to it." I asked him, "Do you worry that you're dying without

God?" because I know that this is an issue for a lot of religious AIDS patients. "Do you feel that God is punishing you, and that's why you're sick?" He answered, "No, I don't. I think I misused my sexuality, as a lot of people do in different ways, and I'm paying the price for that, and it's a high price. But I don't feel I'm dying without God. Just the opposite. The only good thing about my illness is that I learned that something is true which I could only have hoped was true before—that God loves and forgives people no matter how much they've messed up their lives. My main source of comfort is that God has not turned away from me.

"For six years as a priest," he continued, "and for many more years before that, I tried to be perfect so that God would love me, so that God would *have* to love me because I was doing everything right. But I couldn't be perfect, and it frightened and frustrated me because I thought that maybe I wasn't good enough for God to love. Every time I gave in to temptation, every time I told a lie to cover myself, I was afraid that God was as contemptuous of my weakness as I was of myself. But it's a funny thing. Now that I have AIDS and I'm dying, I'm not afraid anymore. Now that God knows who I really am and I don't have to struggle to impress Him anymore. I can be at peace. I feel more tranquil than I've felt for a long time."

He looked at me and said, "I don't have very long to live. I'll be leaving this hospital soon because there is nothing more they can do for me. I hope my congregation won't judge me and reject me for my homosexuality, because I have one more sermon I have to preach so that

215

what I've learned here won't die with me. It's very important for me to tell them what I've learned, that God knows how flawed and imperfect we are, and He loves us anyway."

That was in March of 1986. I've learned since that he died six months later. Where did we get the idea that we have to be perfect to be worthy of love and acceptance? Did we get it from our parents, who had such lofty goals for us, who always wanted us to do better and make the most of ourselves? Did we get it from our teachers, whose method of instruction was to spend more time pointing out what we did wrong than praising us for what we got right? Did we get it from the rabbis and religious leaders of our youth, who emphasized the seriousness of whatever moral and ritual infractions we were capable of when we were children, and taught us that every little deed counted? Whatever its roots, we certainly seem to have gotten the idea that to be good, we had to try to be perfect.

That's why it's so hard for us ever to admit that we're wrong. That's why we instinctively feel the need to defend ourselves when we are criticized. It's like the bumper sticker that reads "The man who can smile when things are going badly has just thought of somebody to blame." We think we have to win every argument, justify every mistake, defuse every criticism, because if we ever admitted that we were wrong, we'd be less than perfect and people wouldn't love us. And the result is, we become stubborn, defensive, always insisting that the problem is somebody else's fault. And if you think about it, what is so lovable about that?

The person who feels he always has to be perfect may secretly feel as I suspect that Episcopal priest in Baltimore used to feel, that if people really knew him, they wouldn't like him. On the political scene, who impresses us more as a leader who is mature and has it all together" the person who denies he was ever wrong, who has to Insist that he never made a mistake, who blames his staff, the press, his political enemies, or the person who can handle the admission that he is not perfect?

This is a rule for family arguments too. The person who cannot admit a mistake, who always has to be right, may think he or she is showing strength, wisdom, control. In point of fact, what he is showing is weakness and fear, the fear that if he confessed to being fallible, if it became known that he wasn't perfect, people would no longer love him. We feel we have to *demand* love by making the case that we are entitled to it on grounds of perfection, rather than let the other person give it to us as a free gift. That's why I suggested in a sermon recently that the four most religious words in the English language are "I may be wrong," and that in a power struggle between parent and child, between husband and wife, the first one to use those words "I may be wrong" wins the argument, because he or she has been able to outgrow the immature need to win every point.

That's what scares me about some of the fundamentalist preachers on television and elsewhere. Their position is that if the Bible is ever wrong on one detail— whether the world was really created in six days, or how long Methuselah lived, or whether Joshua really made the sun stand still—then it's a totally worthless book. It has to be perfect or it's no good at all. Behind it is the attitude that something, or somebody, has to be perfect in order to be taken seriously.

That's why one of the most wonderful things that ever happens to us is to find out, as the dying minister in Baltimore found out and found such peace in discovering, that you can be less than perfect and still be loved. It's not that our sins and mistakes don't matter. They matter very much. They have consequences in our lives and in the lives of people around us. But they're not enough to shatter the relationship between us and God, or between us and other people. Where did we ever get the idea that love means admiring someone for being perfect? Just the opposite; love means accepting someone in full awareness of his or her imperfection. Love is blind only for teenagers with crushes. Because young people haven't learned to compromise and to handle ambiguity, they are always looking for someone perfect, perhaps as a way of saying, "If somebody perfect likes me, then I must be pretty perfect too." That's why they are so sensitive if you point out the faults of the person they think they are in love with. But God isn't a teenager, and neither are most of us, and for us, love is not blind. Love is open-eyed and forgiving.

One of the things Yom Kippur comes to do is precisely this: to wear down our defenses. We fast for twenty-four hours. We spend the entire day in prayer. We repeat the prayers over and over again, "*al chet she—chattanu l'fanecha*, for the sin we have committed before You," almost like an interrogator browbeating a witness, until finally, through a combination, of physical and emotional weariness, we stop denying, we stop defending ourselves, we stop making excuses and pretending that the prayers are just words. We admit that we were weak, superficial, selfish, confused about what was really important. And the moment we do that, something unexpected happens, something very surprising. We don't feel humiliated, exposed, and put down. We feel relieved. We feel clean and strong. All that energy we had been putting into rationalizing and justifying ourselves is free to be used to do other things. It's the psychological equivalent of the budget debate in Congress. If you don't have to put most of your resources into defense, because you no longer think you're about to be attacked, then you can use them in other, more productive ways. In shul as at home, the person who says "I was wrong," not as a tactic but in a moment of honest self-confrontation, doesn't lose; he wins.

For as long as I can remember, I have been taught, and I've taught you, that on Yom Kippur, first you have to forgive the people around you, and only then could you ask God to forgive you. And I've always found that a hard thing to do. Some years ago, for the first time, I realized that the tradition had it backward. It really works the other way around. First, you have to feel forgiven. You have to feel that you're okay, you're a good, acceptable person even if you do some things wrong. And only then, after you've been liberated from the burden of trying to be perfect, of defending and justifying yourself at every point, only then do you feel empowered to forgive others.

There is a conversation I've had with at least thirty members of this congregation, one at a time and almost word for word the same conversation each time. People tell me that they feel like failures despite the fact that they've worked hard at their jobs and at raising their families all their lives, because they didn't live up to their parents' expectations for them. Their parents wanted them to do better at school, to be more successful. I ask them, "Did it ever occur to you that your parents were kind of mixed up, that they had problems of their own, and that's why they had these unrealistic dreams for you?" Maybe your father needed you to become a success because he felt he was a failure. Maybe your mother constantly criticized your boyfriends because it was important to her that your marriage turn out better than hers did. But that's *their* problem. I know that when you were small, they seemed so big and strong and smart, but you're grown-up now. You don't have to see yourself as they saw you, because they may have seen you wrong."

My colleague Rabbi Harold Schulweis of Los Angeles says that there is a distinctively Jewish form of child abuse. It's called being disappointed. So many people I meet are burdened by the feeling that they disappointed their parents after all their parents did for them, and have trouble accepting the notion that their parents set themselves up for disappointment with their unrealistic dreams. But that's their problem, not ours.

We can love our parents, we can honor them as we are commanded to, and we can still see that they were sometimes selfish, small-minded, distracted by other problems, but none of those are unforgivable sins. As parents, they were amateurs in a game where even professionals commit errors; how much perfection could we have expected from them? They were unrealistic if they expected us to be perfect. We are equally unrealistic if we carry around the notion that they were perfect, that anytime they criticized us, they were right.

I meet people who are still arguing with their parents, still looking for approval, for an apology. In some cases, the parents are elderly, even senile. In some cases, the parents have been dead for thirty years, and the daughter is still trying to get them to smile and say to her, "You're a good girl." I ask those people, "Why is it so important to you? Can you accept the idea that if your father never told you he loved you, it's not because you're not lovable. It's because *he* had trouble saying those words, probably because of the way his parents raised him and the circumstances of his childhood, and if we had all the facts, we could probably trace the blame all the way back to Abraham, Isaac, and Jacob, but really what difference would it make?"

When our parents criticize us, it's hard for us not to feel attacked and to become defensive, even if we've done nothing wrong and their demands are unreasonable. But suppose that instead of seeing their words as an attack on us, we could learn to see those words as their problem, as an expression of their neediness. Suppose that instead of responding in our own minds by saying, "I wish they would get off my back and stop making me feel guilty." We learned to say, "I understand what makes them act like that, and I forgive them for it," which is what we picture God saying about us on Yom

Kippur. Suppose we could give them the permission to be flawed, to be weak and human and unreasonable, as God gives us permission to be, but we could love them anyway because we've learned that you don't have to be perfect to earn somebody's love.

When we have gone through the Yom Kippur experience, then we can share that feeling of forgiveness, not only with our parents but with our children as well. We can let go of the notion that our children have to be perfect in order for us to love them. We will no longer see their failures as reflecting on us, and so we will be able to respond to their problems, their shortcomings, in a spirit of support and compassion, rather than disappointment and blame.

On Rosh HaShanah, I introduced the Torah reading, the story of God's commanding Abraham to offer his son Isaac as a sacrifice, with the suggestion that Isaac may have been a retarded child. He was born to elderly parents. He seems to have been a curiously passive figure, never doing anything himself but having things done to him and for him. He is the only man in the entire Bible whose parents worry about his getting married. If we make that assumption, then the story of the sacrifice of Isaac is no longer a story about Abraham's unquestioning obedience to God, and it's not about rejecting human sacrifice. It's a story about the ambivalence we all feel when we find out that our children are not perfect.

We want children not only to provide us with immortality and support us in our old age. We want them to redeem us from our failures, to be the successes we never were, the top student, the best athlete, the most popular girl in class. They will make us look good. How else do you explain the emotional involvement of parents in Little League ballgames, or the number of cars (including mine) that advertise where somebody's son or daughter goes to college? When our children surprisingly turn out to be a lot like us, doing some things pretty well and some things pretty badly but not world class at anything, or when they turn out to have physical or emotional problems, we get confused. We're no longer sure exactly how we feel, about them. We love them, we hurt for them, but at another level we can't help saying to ourselves that this is not what we bargained for. Maybe that is why Abraham thought he heard the voice of God telling him to sacrifice Isaac. It is only when we learn to accept our children as people in their own right, and not as Instruments of correcting our flaws or enhancing our image, that we can forgive them for being only human and love them for who they are.

If you have been to Jerusalem, you probably remember that the southern gate to the Old city, the one closest to the Kotel, is known today as the Lions' Gate. It used to have another name. It used to be called the Dung Gate, *Sha'ar HaAshpot*, the Gate of Filth. The reason usually given for that name is that, during the years the Old City was in Turkish or Arab hands, they would dump garbage at that gate, to make it harder for the Jews who wanted to go to the Kotel, to the Wailing Wall. But among the legends of Old Jerusalem, there is another explanation for that name, one I like better. It teaches that Jewish pilgrims would come to Jerusalem from all over the world to pray at the wall. They would come on foot across the desert. By the time they reached the gates of the city, their feet would be covered by mud and dirt. They didn't want to defile the Temple Mount by entering the city in that condition, so they would wash all the mud and filth off their feet at that southern gate.

We stand tonight at the gate leading to a New Year. We want to enter it clean and undefiled. So we ask Yom Kippur to wash us clean of all those old habits and resentments—the need always to be right; the feeling that we have to be perfect; the fear that no one will love us if they find out we did something wrong; the anger we feel at parents and children, husbands and wives who have problems that we can't solve, and we resent them for making us feel incompetent because we can't solve their problems when all they really want from us is our love and acceptance, not some magic wand. Throughout the past year, we have been burdened by those feelings and that's why the year wasn't as good as it might have been. Only if we wash ourselves clean of those resentments, those expectations, those fears, only then can we walk through the gate and claim the good New Year that awaits us.

TIME STANDS STILL

In 1992, Alan Lightman published a fascinating little book called *Einstein's Dreams*. The idea behind the book is that in 1905, Albert Einstein was working out his theory of relativity, which would revolutionize the way we think about time. He was so obsessed with it that at night he would dream about different worlds where time worked differently than it did in our universe.

For example, he dreams of a world where time runs backward, where people grow younger day by day, till they become infants and disappear into their mothers' wombs. He dreams of a world where time runs in circles, and everything that ever happened happens again after a certain interval. He dreams of a world where time passes more slowly at higher elevations, so that rich people build their houses on mountaintops and live on the top floors of those houses, so that time will pass more slowly and they will live a few hours longer than they would at sea level. But the world that stayed with me most after I had finished the book is a world where time stands still and nothing ever changes, where people have the power to make time stand still.

Young children can't understand that. For them, time passes too slowly. They would love to be able to hurry it up, to be a year older, to reach the next milestone already, to date, to drive, to graduate. They can hardly wait for the new year. But for the rest of us, time passes all too quickly. Has it really been a whole year since we celebrated the High Holy Days last time?

The author of *Einstein's Dreams* writes that the people who make the pilgrimage to the center of time are twofold: those who are in love, and those who have children. And we understand him. There is a part of us that is deeply gratified by our children's growing up, that thrills to every new achievement. But there is also a part of us that knows what the passing of time will do to that relationship. The child who hugs us and needs us and dotes on our praise and makes us feel so smart and so irreplaceable today will evolve into the surly adolescent who slams doors and tells us how little we understand about life. The youngster who wakes up across the hall from us every morning will grow up and go off to college and make a life for himself or herself in another state. And part of us wants to say, "But it's so good now, why does it have to change? Why can't it just stay like this?'

Who travels to the still point in time? Parents with children and people in love. In our world, time moves on and we worry that time may not be kind to us or to the people we love. We're afraid that during the New Year, more of our conversations with our parents, our husbands, our wives will have to do with aches and pains and symptoms and doctors' appointments. And we want to say, "I'm not asking that things be the way they were when I was young, but could we just keep them the way they are now and not get any worse? Could we somehow make time stand still and not let the New Year come and take anything away from me?" What after all is Netaneh Tokef, the prayer that is the emotional highlight of this day, if not a collective articulation of our fears about what the New Year might bring: "It is determined on Rosh HaShanah and confirmed on Yom Kippur, who shall live and who shall die, who by sword and who by ill-ness ..." And we hear ourselves saying, "If those are the coming attractions for the New Year, I'm not sure that's a movie I want to stay for."

We worry about our jobs, about our ability to keep on earning a living, in a world where things change so fast. Companies merge, companies downsize, compa-nies move to another state. People's tastes change and they stop buying what was popular a year ago. So many things remind us that the foundations we've built our lives on, at home and at work, are a lot more fragile and a lot more vulnerable than we would like to think.

But one of the messages of Rosh HaShanah is that there is no stopping time, no way of making it stand still. Inexorably the New Year arrives and whether we like it or not, we have to tear the page off the calendar and go on to the next one.

Do you remember the legend of Faust, the man who sold his soul to the Devil in exchange for happiness in this life? The exact terms of the deal were that, if he ever found himself saying "Let this moment linger; it is so good," then the Devil could have his soul. When I read *Faust* in college, I thought I understood what that meant. I thought Faust was saying, "If I could just have one moment when I could say 'This is great, it doesn't get any better than this,' it would be worth my soul just to be that happy." But as I get older, and I remember that Goethe was nearly eighty when he finished writing *Faust*, I wonder if it might really mean something else. I wonder if Faust was saying, "I would give my soul for myself for the ability to make time stand still, the ability to take a moment and freeze it and never let it change, never let time come and take away that good feeling." And I wonder if the author of *Faust* was saying that the person who tries to make time stand still and keep the world from changing, that person loses his soul.

I've been trying to teach for thirty years that religion means more than God taking attendance on Saturday mornings and checking on whether we've obeyed certain strange rules. Religion is the way we deal with the most basic issues of our lives, making sure we don't have to deal with them alone and sharing with us the wisdom of a hundred generations of thinking about those issues. If one of our basic concerns as we grow a year older is this wish that we could make time stand still because we are afraid of the future, afraid of what change will do to us, to our families, to our world, what answers does Judaism have for us?

Basically Judaism tells us not to be afraid of the future, not because it guarantees the future will be good to us but because it wants to reassure us that we have the resources, the personal and the communal resources, to cope with whatever the future has in store. Judaism's promise is not that it can keep us safe, but that it can make us strong, strong enough to overcome whatever the New Year may bring.

It would tell us first not to be afraid of change because much of what changes, changes for the better. Not all change is loss; not all growth is malignant growth. I had occasion last spring to speak in a synagogue in Brooklyn, just a few blocks away from where I grew up. As I drove past the streets with the familiar names of my childhood, I found myself mourning the disappearance of that world 1 grew up in, a world of neighborhood shopping, flourishing synagogues on every block, safe subways, academically challenging public schools, and the lights of Ebbets Field visible from our front porch during the baseball season. I found myself wishing there were some way 1 could have frozen time in the early 1950s and prevented that neighborhood from deteriorating into the decrepit, crime-ridden slum it has become.

But as I thought about it over the following few days, I realized I probably would not have wanted to go back to the future even if I could. First of all, it would have meant canceling out everything I've done in my life since then. But more than that, yes, the corner grocer knew your name and would extend credit if you were short on cash. But the canned goods were dusty and the milk was one day away from turning sour and you didn't have the choice of products you have today. And for a nickel, you could ride the subway, but getting out of the city was a long ordeal over poor roads by car, and plane travel was about as common as space travel today. And if you got sick, there was so much less that doctors could do for you, and the air was so polluted that you had to wipe a layer of grime off the windowsill every morning. And mothers were expected to stay home with their children, or if they worked, they could be secretaries or schoolteachers and not much more than that. A lot has changed from that Brooklyn neighborhood of forty years ago that I remember so fondly, but a lot of the change has been for the better, and if some Faustian bargain had given me the power to make time stand still in 1955, it would have been a sin against humanity to have done that. Judaism would remind us that change can be scary because it represents leaving the familiar and stepping out into something new. Judaism begins with Abraham leaving the home he grew up in for an unknown destination. It is the story of a band of slaves leaving Egypt for a life they can't imagine, and being so anxious at the prospect that every now and then, they are tempted to call it off and go back to Egypt.

Judaism understands that change is often painful, but that not all pain is bad. Sometimes the pain we feel is the result of growing and stretching. A colleague of mine remembers the day he took his daughter for her first day of kindergarten. As he left her there, anxious and fearful and trying hard not to cry (though his daughter was fine), and closed the door behind him, because it was the High Holy Day season and he was writing his sermons, he thought of the symbolism of doors closing, ending one chapter of our lives and beginning a new one, and how we would never grow if we were afraid to close doors behind us, to leave the familiar and move into the unknown.

I remember telling a member of the congregation who was having problems with a teenager that giving birth to an adolescent can be as painful as giving birth to a newborn child. Cutting the strings that bind a growing child to his or her parents can be painful surgery for both parties, and there are moments when we might be tempted to shy away from the pain, to not grow up because it's safe at home and so scary out there. But Judaism commands us to begin the New Year by rereading the story of Adam and Eve on the first Sabbath of the cycle, how God decreed that because we had gained knowledge of Good and Evil, because we now knew what was right and what was wrong in a way that other creatures could not know, we would find being a parent more painful than any other creature does. And we understand that like Adam and Eve, we have to be wise enough to let go, and like Abraham, our children have to be brave enough to go forth.

But more than anything else, Judaism speaks to those of us who might be tempted to make time stand still, and it says to us: "Don't be afraid." Don't be afraid, not because things won't change that much in the coming year. They may change dramatically. And not because the change won't hurt. It may hurt. But don't be afraid of change because you're strong enough to handle it, and your religion is one of the things that makes you strong enough to handle it.

If the prayer Netaneh Tokef is our great cry of apprehension, of concern over what the New Year might take away from us, what is the prayer book's answer to that cry? It comes in seven words of Hebrew at the end of Netanch Tokef, "*ut'shuvah ut'fillah ut'zedakah ma'avirin et ro'a ha'zerah*, Repentance, prayer and charity avert the severity of the decree." Notice how carefully that line is phrased. It doesn't say that repentance, prayer and charity avert the decree, that being religious will keep bad things from happening to you. If it said that, people would have noticed hundreds of years ago that it wasn't true. It says that they avert the *severity* of the decree. Bad things may happen to you but they won't hurt as much, because you will have learned to see yourself and to see the world around you in a way that keeps those misfortunes in perspective.

Prayer can make the bitter moments of the New Year hurt less. I remember years ago, a man came up to me and said, "Rabbi, you know that since my father died, I've been coming to the minyan every night to say Kaddish. For the next month or so, I'll be traveling a lot on business. Some nights I'll be on a plane when it's time for the evening service. Some nights I'll be in a small town where there is no synagogue. Would it be a sin if I just said Kaddish by myself in my room?"

I told him, "No, I think it would be the right thing to do. I know how important it is for you to say Kaddish for your father every day. Just don't lose sight of the fact that when you say Kaddish with a congregation, two very important things happen that don't happen when you say it by yourself. First, the other members of the congregation give you strength by welcoming you, by saying Amen to your prayer, and because several of them are mourners as well, by reminding you that you're not the only one this has happened to.

"And the second thing is, you give them strength. When they see you in shul, when they hear the one person who has the most right to be angry at God get up and affirm God, that does something for them. It banishes their fear that when they lose someone they love, they won't be able to handle it. It teaches them something about the resiliency of the human soul in the face of tragedy."

The discipline of prayer can't protect us from pain and sorrow. It can't prevent people from getting old, from getting sick. But it can avert the *severity* of the decree. It can make it hurt less.

And if we come to understand what *teshuvah*, repentance, really means, it can help us deal with adverse fate as well. I think the word "repentance" makes a lot of us uncomfortable because it has connotations of beating our breasts and groveling and saying, "I'm no good, it's all my fault." But that's wrong. Teshuvah, repentance in Judaism, is really the opposite of that. It asks us to say, "Yes, I've done some things wrong, as everybody does. But that's not the essential me. The real me is capable of being good and strong and brave most of the time."

The unexpected success of the Red Sox this summer had me remembering the last time the Red Sox were in the World Series, in 1986. 1 don't know if you remember it, but we had problems starting Kol Nidre on time that year. The Red Sox were in a playoff game in California. If they lost, their season would be over. And people didn't want to leave for shul until the game had been decided. They were losing with two out in the ninth inning, when

California pitcher Donnie Moore gave up a home run to Dave Henderson that cost California the ballgame. Donnie Moore never got over that one mistake. He blamed himself for his team's losing. He kept wishing he could turn back the clock, do that one moment over again and do it differently. Two years later, he was traded. A year after that, he was out of baseball. Then, hopelessly depressed, he took his own life. He could never forgive himself for doing that one thing wrong.

Now, contrast that with something that happened two and a half years ago in a college basketball game. A nineteen-year-old sophomore from Michigan, Chris Webber, made a mental mistake that cost his team the national championship. But unlike Donnie Moore, he didn't lose faith in himself. He said, "That was a dumb thing to do, but it doesn't change the fact that I'm a good player." A year later, Chris Webber was the NBA's Rookie of the Year.

If we root our lives in goodness, in honesty, in charity, then even if the bad things that come our way are the result of bad decisions on our part, our sense of ourselves as good people will diminish the severity of what happens to us. And if we form the habit of charity, of feeling the pain of other people and wanting to do something to help them, then our own problems will hurt us less, not only because we will be aware of how much suffering there is in the world, but because we will have learned to see ourselves as people with the power to do something about it. We will see ourselves as people who act, not as passive victims.

The synagogue is not a place to escape from the real world. The synagogue is not a place for people who want things to remain the same and never change. The synagogue is where you learn what the world is really about, what really matters in this world, and how you armor yourself against the dangers the world poses.

And on Rosh HaShanah, the synagogue's message is "Don't be afraid." Don't be afraid of change, of not being able to control things that are so important to you. Not because life guarantees happy endings, but because the right kind of life leaves you equipped to cope with whatever ending comes along. Don't be afraid that life may hurt, not because we can assure you it won't hurt, but because faith and friends and self-esteem will make you strong enough to take it. On Rosh HaShanah, the synagogue asks us to give up our fantasy that we can make time stand still. It asks us to give up our illusion that what we have today, we will have forever. And it asks us to give up our fear of the future. In their place, it offers us the way of *teshuvah, tefillah utzedakah*, the way of confidence, prayer, and generosity, so that as the door of the old year closes behind us, we can enter the door that opens for us, and we can enter it unafraid.

SCHINDLER'S LIST

When I sit down every summer to start writing my sermons for the High Holy Days, I often begin by asking myself, "What was the most important Jewish story of the past year?" For the year 1995, I would suggest that the big story was the appearance, the success, and the honors heaped on Steven Spielberg's movie *Schindler's List*. I think it was an important movie for Jews, not because it documented the fact that the Holocaust really happened and how terrible it was. People who have a psychological need to deny the Holocaust aren't going to be changed by one movie. And besides, I sometimes think that the Holocaust is too much a part of the Jewish public image. I would rather people admired us for what we do to change the moral climate in America than feel sorry for us because of what happened to other Jews in Hitler's Europe. I would like to see a second museum in Washington, D.C., celebrating what Jews have done for the world, to stand alongside the Holocaust Memorial Museum and its chronicle of what the world did to us.

And I don't think *Schindler's List* is important because of what it represents in terms of Spielberg's coming to terms with his Jewishness, although if you've read the story, it's a fascinating one. Steven Spielberg was raised in a series of small towns where he was often the only Jew in his school. Children made fun of him for being Jewish, and in response he retreated into a private world of fantasy and imagination. *Star Wars*, *E.T.*, and *Jurassic Park* are the result of that boy's finding the world of his imagination more gratifying than the real world. But *Schindler's List* is the product of a Spielberg who has finally grown up, accepted his Jewishness as one of the givens of his life, and accepted the world as the flawed, imperfect place it is. Like Alfred Dreyfus whose trial began exactly one hundred years ago, like Jonah whose story we read on Yom Kippur afternoon, Spielberg learned that you can't run away from who you are.

But to my mind, all of these aspects of the movie are secondary. The real importance of *Schindler's List* is that it tells the story of a far-from-perfect person who becomes a much better person. And this is the Rosh HaShanah story, how flawed people, people who are not saints and are not religiously gifted, can become better.

If Rosh HaShanah does not leave us motivated to change, to do things differently in our lives, and if Yom Kippur does not leave us feeling cleansed, then we are wasting our time. Then all this effort to set up extra chairs and put up the tent and give out tickets, and for you to take three days off from work, will not have been worth it. And we need the story of Oskar Schindler to convince us that it *is* possible.

When we first meet Oskar Schindler, he is a rather unpleasant person. He makes his living by smuggling, offering bribes, and taking advantage of other people's misfortune, and in his spare time, he cheats on his wife. He is a self-indulgent schemer with a weakness for good food, fine wine, and attractive women. But over the course of the movie, he changes, not into a saint but into an imperfect person who devotes his strength and his fortune to saving lives. And the first lesson of the movie is, if somebody like Oskar Schindler can change and become a better person, so can any one of us. We don't start out as depraved as he did, and we don't have to reach the same level of self-sacrifice he did, but we have at least the same resources for changing that he had. The ultimate atheism is not to deny God's existence, but to deny God's power to help us grow and improve. And the ultimate blasphemy against God's world is to utter the words "That's the way I am, and there's nothing I can do about it."

How does a person change? What motivates us to drop a bad habit and substitute a good one? Being nagged to change doesn't do it, and neither does the abstract intellectual knowledge that what we are doing is wrong. It takes more than that. I'd like to offer you three scenarios of how a person can be motivated to change his life, not necessarily in big dramatic ways, but in a lot of little ways, and that can be enough to make a difference. And the first pattern is the Oskar Schindler pattern.

We change because we are horrified by a vision of where we will end up if we don't. This is what happened to Schindler. He may have been a crook and an adulterer, but he wasn't a murderer. He wasn't a sadist, a torturer. When he sees the Nazis, his drinking companions and business partners, killing people without remorse, hunting down and murdering children, something inside him says, "No, that's not how people are supposed to behave." And in that moment, he turns from working with them to working against them.

I believe that there is in every one of us, in every normal human being, an instinctive sense of injustice, an emotional response that certain things are wrong. It's not an intellectual awareness that something is against the law. It's an emotional response that people have no right to treat each other this way, whether there is a law against it or not. This is what snaps in Oskar Schindler and causes him to turn his life around.

Our moment of transformation doesn't have to be as dramatic as that, but it can be structurally similar. We look around at people we know, people we read about, and hear a voice inside us say, "I don't want to end up like that. I may be inclined to do some of the things they do, I may find myself at times envying them, but if that's where it leads, it's not worth it."

We see people advancing their own agenda by *using* other people and discarding them when they're used up, and we see them end up lonely, friendless, and unloved. We see them mess up their families out of false priorities and misplaced ambition. We see people lie because the truth would be embarrassing, and before long people catch on to them, and even when they tell the truth, they are not believed. And we say to ourselves, "I would sooner face the embarrassment and count on there being forgiveness in the world, rather than end up like that." We see families go from being a unit to being a collection of individuals eating and sleeping at the same address but each with his own agenda, unrelated to one another except by genetics and geography. We hear voices, sometimes in the name of psychology, sometimes even in the name of religion, telling us that we'll never really be grown up until we break our bonds to our family, telling us that our goal in life is to make the most of our own lives and let other people worry about theirs. But we see where that leads and we decide that that isn't somewhere we want to go. We remember the words of the Talmud: "Saying 'what's mine is mine and what's yours in yours' is what caused the destruction of the wicked city of Sodom." We say to ourselves, "To belong to another person is the most fulfilling feeling in the world. I feel sorry for people who don't have it. Why would anyone who is lucky enough to have that let it slip away?"

There was a time when religion would try to motivate people to control their behavior by conjuring up images of the tortures of hell, portraying the punishments of the damned. We don't have to do that today. All we have to do is ask people to read the last chapter of the lives of public figures and people we've known, people whom we might have envied until we saw how their story turned out, selfish people, shallow, people, unscrupulous people, and absorb the lesson: they may have had fun getting there, but God help me, I don't want to end up where they did.

The second pattern is the opposite of the first. I don't have a name for it, because some of the names that come to mind are names of people who are in the congregation today and I don't want to embarrass them. Instead of recoiling from evil and saying, "I don't want to be like that," we experience a moment of being good, of being generous, of being in control of ourselves, and it feels so good that we hear ourselves saying, "I would like to feel like that more often."

It is a cornerstone of my religious faith that, just as our bodies are made so that certain foods and certain ways of living are healthier for us and others harm us, in the same way, our souls are made so that certain ways of living are healthy for our souls and other ways are toxic. I believe that human beings are meant to be truthful, helpful, cheerful, and generous. When we do those things, it feels right. An hour of visiting a lonely person, helping a sick friend, volunteering for a cause we believe in gives us the same high, the same rush of endorphins, as an hour's workout at the gym. You deliver the left-over food from a party to an organization that feeds the homeless, you attend a class, you say No to temptation and hold back an angry, hurtful remark, and you feel "Yes, this is the way a person is supposed to feel."

There are men and women sitting here this morn-ing who had no background of synagogue involvement when they were growing up, and had no expectation of serious involvement when they first joined Temple Israel. But something happened—you came to a service, maybe for a bar mitzvah, you were saying Kaddish for a year, you attended a meeting that sounded interesting and somebody invited you to serve on a committee— and that's where it all started. You enjoyed it and came back for more, until temple involvement became an unexpectedly important part of your family's life. And when somebody tried to tell you they appreciated what you were doing, you told them, "I get more out of it than I give." And do you know something? You're right.

Some years ago, they did an experiment at Duke University Medical Center in North Carolina, a study of Type A personalities. You know, the impatient, hard-driving, success-oriented person. Their hypothesis was that being so driven and so intent on succeeding would cause these people to have stress-related problems in their cardiovascular system. They rounded up a couple hundred unmistakable Type As and examined them, and found that some were sick and some were healthy. And this seemed to be the key: If you were an ambitious Type A because you enjoyed the challenge of making things happen, of seeing a successful operation and knowing that you helped bring it about, you'll be just fine. In fact, you'll probably be healthier than most people. But if you are a hyperactive Type A because you believe it's a jungle out there, because you believe that everybody is out to cheat you unless you're clever enough to cheat them first, then your cardiovascular system will pay the price for that, because that's not how human beings were designed to function.

Two months ago, Suzette and I spent a week in Rio de Janeiro, where I had been invited to give a series of talks at the local synagogue. Rio is one of the world's most beautiful cities. The only problem is, you can't go out of your hotel to enjoy it. There is so much crime, against natives and tourists alike, that it drains much of the joy from the experience of being there. The only time we could walk around safely was during the World Cup soccer games, when even the robbers were indoors watching television.

And my reaction was, "How can people live like this?" Human beings were not meant to see each other as threatening, as enemies. It corrodes the soul. To go into a business meeting, to walk into an automobile showroom, to sit down with an insurance adjuster with the mentality that you have to lie to protect yourself because the other person is going to lie to take advantage of your gullibility—that does something to a person. Inevitably it ends up affecting the way you talk to your friends, to your children. You end up calculating the effect of your words instead of speaking your heart freely. I sometimes suspect that some of the curative power of psychotherapy and of a really true friendship is that it permits you to let down your guard and speak honestly.

How does a person bring himself to change? You experience something, in the way you spend your time, your money, your energy, that makes you feel good and clean, that connects you with other people in ways that enhance the humanity of both of you. And you say, "You know, there is no reason why I can't do that more often."

The third pattern for change is what I would call the Alfred Nobel pattern. I don't know if you know very much about the man behind the Nobel Prizes. He was a chemist, and he made his fortune as the inventor of dynamite. He licensed his invention to governments, became a rich man, and retired to a life of leisure. One day, his older brother died and one newspaper got the story wrong and printed Alfred's obituary instead. Nobel had the rare experience of reading his own obituary while he was still alive, and seeing what it was that people would remember him for.

It began, "Dr. Alfred Nobel, who became rich by finding a way to kill more people faster than ever before, died yesterday at the age of..." He said to himself, "No, that's not the way I want to be remembered," and he took his entire fortune to establish the Nobel Prizes for people who have done things to help humanity. And it worked. Very few people associate his name with dynamite; hundreds of millions of people associate it with the prestige of the Nobel Prizes.

For us, the confrontation may not be as dramatic, but it's very similar. One of the things that happens to us on Rosh HaShanah is that we confront our mortality. We're reminded that we're not going to live forever. Sooner or later we all fall into that category of being remembered for the kind of person we were. We come to Netaneh Tokef, with its image of the books being open and all our deeds recorded, and for some of us, it will be embarrassing to read them: the pettiness, the falsehoods, the unnecessary arguments, the feuds prolonged that we could have ended. Is that what we want written next to our names?

We come to shul on Rosh HaShanah, not to grovel before God and beg Him for another year of life. I hope you don't believe that that's how it works. We come to be reminded of the preciousness of time, that years seem so much shorter now than they did when we were young, and to be reminded of the urgency of fashioning a life we can be proud of.

Oskar Schindler had his list, and it was literally a Sefer Chaim, a Book of Life in which it was recorded who shall live and who shall die. And if your name appeared on his list, you were literally inscribed in the Book of Life for another year. And we have our lists, very different lists from Schindler's. We have lists of names of people we belong to, people we share our lives with, people with whom we fashion a life of loving and caring and meaning. We have our lists of things we care about, lists of things we wish were different about us, and lists of things we'd like to be remembered for. And on Rosh HaShanah, when we come to shul and are reminded of the fragility of life and the urgency of change, we pause to reorganize those lists, to make sure that the things we want to be remembered for are at the top. And if we have a list of things that embarrass us, things we would rather not have people associate with our names, we have the power to change them, not to change the past, but to change the future, just as Oskar Schindler and Alfred Nobel each forged a new identity that completely overshadowed the old one, so that we remember them for who they became, not for who they used to be, so that a person can say, "Those other things? That wasn't me who did them; that was somebody else by the same name." Because when we restructure our values, as Schindler did, as Nobel did, as some of the people sitting around you this morning have done, we each become a new person, no longer burdened by the record we wrote in years past.

May you all be granted a year of life in the New Year just begun, and may you use that year of life wisely, so that next year will see us all gathered here again, comfortable with who we are and confident about whom we are becoming.

THE WORST SIN

What would you say is the worst sin that a person can commit? Yom Kippur after all is a time to bravely face up to all the things we do wrong, and try to do something about them. If we can't fix everything all at once and we want to start with our most serious failures, where should we start? Of all the things that people are capable of doing wrong, what is the worst?

The Rabbis of the Talmud claim that the worst sin is *Hillul HaShem*, bringing the Name of God into disrepute. For a Jew to act in such a way that other people say, "What kind of religion lets a person get away with that?" is the worst thing we can do, because it not only contaminates your little corner of the world. It shames the entire Jewish people.

The medieval philosophers taught that the worst sin was the repudiation of God, because when you do that, you have no reason to refrain from other sins. The basis of your morality becomes "What can I get away with? Will I be caught and punished?" rather than "Is it right?"

Modern thinkers tend to answer the question in more humanistic, less theological terms. My friend Dennis Prager says that cruelty to another human being is the worst sin a person can commit. Martin Buber, building on an idea of the philosopher Immanuel Kant, taught that the ultimate sin was to *use* another person, to treat someone as a means to an end rather than as an end in himself or herself.

I read each of those definitions, I think about them, and each one persuades me that it's correct. That's about as bad as human behavior ever gets. So I would like to offer my own suggestion, which combines all of the others: *The gravest sin a person can commit is to look at another person and not see the image of God incarnated there.* Rabbi Akiba is quoted in the Talmud as saying that the most important words in the Torah are the statement that God created human beings in His own image. Everything else we do—the way we treat our wives and husbands, parents and children, the way we treat employees and the way we treat strangers, the way we treat people we don't like—everything follows from that one insight: every human being on earth is fashioned in the image of God. The second of the Ten Commandments tells us not to make a graven image of God and worship it, because every human being, and only a human being, is an image of God and deserves to be treated as such.

I don't understand how a person can plant a bomb in a building and kill dozens of people—whether it's in Buenos Aires, Belfast or Beirut—unless first he has rejected the teaching that every one of those victims is an image of God. I don't understand how somebody can shoot or stab another person because he doesn't like that other person's politics, his nationality, his skin color, or even the fact that the other person has more money than he does—unless first he blinds himself to the image of God that he is violating.

My problem with the resurgence of the fundamentalist Christian right in American politics is not that I disagree with them on abortion or homosexuality, or with their efforts to take sex education out of the public schools and put creation science in. In a democracy, that's what you do: you articulate your ideas and you let the voters decide. My problem with the Christian right is that they are so good at hating. So much of their energy is fueled not by devotion to what they believe, but by hatred of the people who disagree with them. This is the poison that the Rush Limbaughs, Pat Buchanans, and Jerry Falwells pour into the stream of American discourse every day, hating and demonizing the people with whom they disagree. It's not just that they can't see the logic of the other person's position. They can't see the humanity of the other person. They don't, recognize the person who disagrees with them as bearing the image of God.

And I'm sorry; to me, that's not religion. Real religion does not teach people to hate. I'm often amused by the spectacle of people who can't read Hebrew being so sure that they know what God wants because they've read it in the Bible. I always thought that religion taught humility, that the four most religious words a person could speak were "I may be wrong," but how often do you hear that from a public figure, whether religious or political, today?

If I were Muslim, I would be deeply embarrassed by so many, things that are being said and done in the name of Islam. From terrorist murders not only of Israelis but of tourists in Egypt and religious moderates in Algeria, to the bombing of the World Trade Center in New York, to the death threats against Salman Rushdie, to the humiliation of women in Iran and North Africa—things are done not only by people who were born Muslims, but by people who claim they are acting in the name of Islam. If decent Muslims are offended by the connection of the words "Muslim" and "terrorist" in the public mind, the reason is not that newspaper editors in New York and movie producers in Hollywood are anti-Muslim. The reason is that terrible things are done in the name of Allah, and nobody speaks out to denounce them. Nobody says that to do these things to a human being is a desecration of the Name of God.

If I were Muslim, I would be embarrassed by the things that are done in the name of Islam. But I'm not Muslim; I'm a Jew. And I'm embarrassed by some of the things that are done in the name of Judaism, by the spectacle of people who should know better losing sight of the image of God in human beings whom they don't like.

A few weeks ago, a colleague of mine called me up and said, "I want to read something to you." He read me a paragraph about how terrible a sin it was to kill another person. I said, "Sure, everybody knows that. Why are you sharing this with me?" He told me he found it in the yearbook of the Yeshiva of Flatbush from some twenty-odd years ago. I asked, "What's so special about that?" and he told me it had been written by Baruch Goldstein, who was responsible for the massacre in the Hebron mosque. What horrifies me about that incident is not just that one person who claimed to be a devout Jew could do such a thing, but that even a handful of religious spokesmen could justify it. How could someone who was an Orthodox Jew justify letting his anger overcome his religious obligation to see other human beings as bearing the image of God?

If you remember the story in the Torah of how Jacob disguises himself as his brother Esau to gain the blessing that was meant for Esau, then you remember that when Esau finds out what happens, he bursts out crying. And the Midrash tells us that God hears the cry of Esau and says that the redemption will not come until the tears of Esau have been dried. If we can't grant the legitimacy of the tears and pain of the Palestinian Esaus, not the legitimacy of their demands but the legitimacy of their pain, we are no better than the those who see every Israeli as a symbol of aggression, not as a living, breathing, hoping, loving human being. If we accept the suffering and death of some people because of what some others did, if we permit ourselves to say, "they deserve it; they did it first and worse," we lose sight of the God-given humanity of other human beings, we delay the redemption, and we commit the most serious sin anyone can commit.

But you don't have to be an international terrorist or an inner-city gangster to be guilty of this worst of sins. If that were the case, it wouldn't be worth giving a sermon about. Members of Hamas and Hezbollah are not in shul this morning, although they have plenty to atone for, and the rest of you don't need to be persuaded that planting bombs in public buildings is wrong. But I think we can be guilty of a milder form of the same transgression, forgetting that every one of the people we deal with is an image of God. We're so ready to dismiss people, to write them off. They have nothing to teach us, they have no claim on us; why should we take them seriously except insofar as they can be useful to us?

You get a message that someone who was supposed to do some work for you has taken ill or has a seriously ill child and won't be able to come. Is your first thought one of compassion for him, or is it of your own inconvenience? If a waitress or store clerk seems distracted or forgetful, is your only response to get annoyed, or does it occur to you that she may have something serious going on in her life that makes it hard for her to keep her mind on her work?

Almost forty-five years ago, I read a short story in a high school English class about the wife of a British colonel in India who was expecting some important company for tea one afternoon. At noon, she looked out and was horrified to see that her gardener had not shown up for work and the front walk was covered with leaves and dirt. When he finally appeared at one o'clock, she tore into him, telling him how unappreciative he was to have such a good job and how easily she could replace him. When she finished, the man looked up at her and said, quietly, "I'm sorry. My little girl died last night and we had to bury her." For the first time, the colonel's lady had to see this gardener not just as someone who was useful to her, someone who showed up to sweep the steps every morning, but as a human being, with family, with pains, with morning, but as a human being, with family, with pains, with hopes and dreams.

Are we capable of encountering a physically handicapped person, a severely retarded person, a mentally disturbed person, a terminally ill person, and recognizing the image of God in that person? Or does our own sense of vulnerability overwhelm the humanity, the divine core of the person we meet? I received a bar mitzvah invitation the other day from a couple I had met ten years ago. They came to see me because they had read my book about bad things happening to good people, and wanted to talk to me about their three-year-old son who had a rare and devastating neurological disease, a form of Tay-Sachs. The boy will turn thirteen later this month. He can't speak, let alone read from the Torah. He can't sit up, let alone stand on the bimah. But they are working out a bar mitzvah celebration for him, because they want their friends and family to recognize and celebrate the fact that inside this crippled body there is a Jewish soul reaching out to God.

Are we capable of seeing people we've had an argument with as bearers of God's image, or does the bitterness obscure the godliness? Can we see our children as bearing God's image, or is it just resemblance to us that we look for? Sometimes we have trouble seeing our children as unique souls on their own, but only as extensions of our needs and wishes. We hurt them by being disappointed when they grow up to have their own agenda that doesn't match ours. I remember sitting and talking with a member of the congregation some years ago about an educational and career choice his twenty-six-year-old daughter was making, of which he disapproved. He kept on saying, "Why is she doing this to me?" I tried to tell him, "She's not doing it to you. She's doing it because she feels it's what she needs to do at this point in her life. That you are her father and feel strongly about it is natural and all to the good. But you've raised her to be an independent person and do her own thing, and you should be proud of the fact that she's doing it."

To see people only in terms of what they do for us robs them of their essential humanity. It means *using* them instead of *meeting* them. To be disappointed in children because they seek to meet their own needs instead of meeting our needs is to blind ourselves to the miracle that a child represents, that out of the love that a husband and wife share, they create a human being who bears the image of the God who gave them the power to create life, and that human being grows up to have a mind and a conscience of her own. What an incredible miracle that is, if we could only rise above our own needs and expectations and be able to see it.

There is one other time when we are vulnerable to the sin of looking at a person and not recognizing the image of God reflected there, and that is every morning when we see ourselves in the mirror. I think one of the most serious sins we commit is not to take ourselves seriously,

There is a scene in the Torah, at the very end of the Book of Genesis, when the patriarch Jacob has come to the end of his life. His son Joseph has come to visit him, and Jacob, like many old people, is reminiscing about the life he led. It was quite a life. In an age when most people never traveled outside of their own communities, Jacob has lived in three countries. He has made and lost fortunes, he has suffered and he has triumphed. But all of that fades, and one memory remains. Jacob remembers that when he was young, God appeared to him and God told him that he would grow up to be a special person. He has never forgotten that. At crucial moments in his life, he harked back to that dream at Bethel and it kept him going.

I suspect that there are a lot of people here who once had a moment like that. Back when we were young, we had an intuition that we were going to do something special without lives. We were going to achieve great things; we were going to make a difference. People would know who we were. But then we got bogged down in getting a job, getting married, raising a family, paying bills. Unlike Jacob, we forgot that vision. Or if we remembered it, we dismissed it as adolescent naïveté, like our daydreams of being a movie star or playing for the Red Sox. And when we did that, we betrayed the image of God that was planted in each of us. When we make the choice, as so many American Jews, have done, as so many Jews in Natick and Framingham have done, not to be serious Jews, we do it not because we don't take God seriously and not because we don't take Judaism seriously. We do it because we don't take *ourselves* seriously, as people who are fashioned in God's image. We ignore the potential every one of us was born with: to grow up to be a real human being, a visible statement of what God stands for, what God would look like if we could see Him.

Judaism is not a bunch of rules we're supposed to obey to please God. That's a child's understanding of life, something we should really have outgrown by this point. Judaism is the science of making your life matter by taking the ordinary and making it holy. Judaism is what you do to save your life from being insignificant. I believe that there is an existential human need for significance, a need to know that our lives matter. People do wonderful things, like giving to charity, and people do desperate things, like trying to assassinate the president, in an effort to reassure themselves that they matter, that they make a difference to the world. And what the Jewish way of life is about more than anything else is a way of filling your life with moments of significance.

Even if you can't sing like Streisand or shoot baskets like Michael Jordan, even if you're not in line to become CEO of a major organization, you can do things that God does. You can take the first half of a weekend and turn it into Shabbat, even as God took the seventh day and sanctified it. You have the same power. You can cleanse the air in your home by the kind of words you use and the kind of words you never use, by the kind of movies you go to and the kind of movies you refuse to go to. You can take the act of eating, which we share with animals, and infuse it with holiness by refusing to eat the way animals eat and choosing to eat the way Jews eat, with rules, with reverence, with an appreciation for the miracle that a meal represents. The gravest sin we can commit is to waste a life. On the last Shabbat of the old year, three days before Rosh HaShanah, we read the words of the Torah "*uvacharta bachavyim*," usually translated as "choose life." A colleague of mine suggested that the real translation of those words is "Get a life." "Get a life" is a phrase that has entered the English language with the connotation of "Don't waste your life just sitting around and living vicariously through other people. Do something with your life. Your life has the potential to be something really special. Don't blow it."

Some lives are wasted on the altar of ethnic hatred and religious intolerance, and we respond in horror to the blasphemy that represents. Some are wasted when people are born into conditions of squalor and violence, so that survival becomes a full-time job with no energy left over for developing one's soul. Some lives are wasted when we try to confine people to serving *our* needs instead of letting their own souls flourish. But more than in any other way, lives are wasted because we just don't care enough. People forget their dreams, people forget their heritage, people give up on themselves and let the noise of the world drown out the voice of God calling out to every one of us to become somebody special, and showing us how to do it.

If we can't fix everything in the world by our efforts and put an end to the killing and the hating, and if we can't fix everything about ourselves all at once, but we want to fix one thing at a time, maybe this is the place to start: to see all people—people we don't like, people we live with, and the face we find in the mirror—as images of God, and to treat them all, especially the one in the mirror, the way the image of God deserves to be treated.

It's Still Special to be Human

This summer, as I began to think about what I wanted to say to you on Yom Kippur. I once again asked myself, "What was the big story of the year that just ended?" And because Yom Kippur is about human fallibility, about human beings making mistakes and learning from their mistakes, I decided that the big story of 1997 was the IBM computer Deep Blue defeating Garry Kasparov in a high-stakes chess match. Millions of people had a rooting interest in the match, most of us (except for a few computer nerds) rooting for Kasparov, whether out of species solidarity or perhaps, as someone once said of auto racing fans, out of a deep desire to see God's creation master Man's creation.

But the machine won, and a lot of us felt diminished by its victory. Here was one more thing that we thought humans were uniquely good at, and it turns out you can build a machine that can do it better. But for me, the computer's victory didn't make it less special to be a human being. One the contrary, it clarified for me what it means to be human. What remains special about being human?

For one thing, so the computer won. But could it enjoy its victory? I suspect the engineers who programmed it were exulting and high-fiving it when their machine won, but did the machine feel anything? No, the whole world of emotion, of joy, of hope, of love, of pride was beyond it. Only people can feel those things, as only people can feel sadness, rejection, depression. And because some of the feelings that humans are uniquely open to are painful feelings, there are a lot of people who are afraid to take off the armor and make themselves vulnerable to feeling anything at all. They are willing to forgo the possibility of feeling joy and hope, to make sure they will never have to feel disappointment and rejection. They go through life anesthetized, numbing themselves against all emotion.

When I first came to this congregation thirty-one years ago and you, the members of the Natick-Framingham Jewish community, began to bring me your problems, I found myself encountering virtually the same problem over and over again. I began to think of it as the "Route 128 Syndrome." There were a lot of men who worked in one of the high-tech electronics firms along Route 128 who, by temperament or training, had learned to be comfortable with numbers that held still as you manipulated them, and uncomfortable with feelings, which tended to be unpredictable and often out of control. They provided *things* for their children, but had trouble connecting with their children emotionally. When a parent died, they couldn't figure out how to mourn, how to grieve. When they had problems in their marriage, their first impulse was to leave rather than try to work out painful conflicts. They were uncomfortable with arguments, with confrontation. These were highly intelligent people, very articulate when they talked about their work (I could never understand them), but on any subject other than their work or local sports teams, there was an emotional flatness to their conversation. Afraid of feelings because they couldn't control them, afraid of feelings because some feelings were painful—if you let yourself need someone, you give that person the power to hurt you and they didn't want to be hurt—they became like the machines they designed, capable of doing wondrous things but not capable of enjoying them.

And yet what is Yom Kippur if not a day of making ourselves vulnerable to painful feelings? We go without food, to prove to ourselves that when we put our minds to it, we can control even the strongest instincts. We offer Yizkor prayers, stirring up some painful memories, painful because we miss people so much, painful because of the unfinished business left behind when they died, but we do it because we understand that part of being who we are involves summoning up those memories. And sometimes it hurts, but we understand how diminished we would be as human beings if we couldn't bring ourselves to do that.

Recently at a speech I was giving, someone asked me, "Doesn't it bother you that the God of the Hebrew Bible is such a wrathful, short-tempered God?" I said, "No, I prefer that to the God of the philosophers, a God incapable of emotion because emotion implies change and passivity." I remember Professor Abraham Heschel telling us in class that the God of Aristotle is the Unmoved Mover, but the God of Israel was the most-moved Mover, a God moved by strong emotions, a God who loved, who cared about us, who grew angry at wickedness, who was offended by disloyalty.

To be a real human being is to be more like God and less like a machine, to be fashioned in the image of God in a way that no other creature is. To be a real human being is to be capable of feeling joy and feeling pain, feeling love and feeling grief, experiencing triumph and experiencing failure. It means being brave enough to take off the armor and make yourself vulnerable to all those feelings.

There is a second lesson to be learned from Deep Blue's victory over Kasparov.

Do you know what else people can do that computers can't? People can make mistakes. That's why we have Yom Kippur every year, because we can predict that between now and next September, each of us will do things we will wish we hadn't done. Each of us will have occasion to be embarrassed by the weakness, the openness to temptation that is an inescapable dimension of our humanity. And each of us will have the opportunity to learn from our mistakes and to grow.

I saw Wendy Wasserstein's new play, *An American Daughter*. Although there is nothing really Jewish about the play, it takes place at the High Holy Day season.

Maybe Ms. Wasserstein, who is Jewish, wanted echoes of the themes of Days of Judgment: "who shall live and who shall die, who shall rise and who shall be brought low." The one Jewish character in the play is going off to a Tashlich service on the afternoon of Rosh HaShanah, the ceremony of casting our sins into a body of flowing water, and tries to explain Tashlich to her non-Jewish friend. She translates it as "the holiday of regrets." I thought that was good. One of the themes of this season, one of the ideas that focuses on what it means to be human, is that only human beings can have something like an annual holiday of regrets.

Making it a religious ceremony is a way of telling us that we don't have to be embarrassed by our regrets, by our failures, our dreams that didn't come true last year and might or might not come true this year. To be genuinely human is to be aware, in a way that no other creature and certainly no mechanical device can be aware, of the gap between what we do and what we know we ought to do, between what we are and what we would like to be.

To be capable of feeling shame, to be capable of knowing that you have done something wrong, is to proclaim your humanity, because that is something that neither a machine nor an animal can do. And to be incapable of feeling shame is to admit that there is something deficient in your humanity.

I think one of the great stories of this past year happened after that tragic incident in Israel when a Jordanian soldier shot and killed seven schoolgirls on a field trip. Do you remember what happened after that? King Hussein of Jordan canceled a European trip and came to Israel to pay condolence calls on the bereaved families and apologize to them in the name of the Jordanian people. He didn't have to do that. He could have had his press secretary grind out a statement deploring the act and distancing himself from it. But he chose to react as a human being and not give the automatic bureaucratic response, and in doing that, he taught us all a lesson in how high a human soul can rise.

Every now and then, I will find myself exposed to a few minutes of daytime television, one of those talk shows where people go on national television and tell the world how messed up their lives are. And I find myself wondering, "What's wrong with those people, that they are not embarrassed by the things they are talking about? What thirst for recognition or notoriety drives them to bare themselves like this without embarrassment?" And the celebrities, the movie stars, the athletes, even the politicians, who seem beyond the reach of shame. It used to be that when a public figure was caught doing something wrong, his response would be "I can't talk about it; I'm too embarrassed." Now the response is "I can't talk about it until my book comes out and I go on television to promote it."

If you remember the opening chapters of the Bible, right after Adam and Eve eat the fruit of the knowledge of good and evil, right after they separate themselves from the rest of the animal kingdom by gaining a knowledge that certain things are right and others wrong, the first thing that happens to them is that they feel shame for being naked. Now, on a literal level, that makes no sense because there is literally no one else in the world to see them in that condition, so why are they embarrassed? But as a symbol of the human condition, as a symbol of what happens when you acquire a sense of good and bad, it makes a lot of sense. To feel shame is to know that there are expectations people have of you that you may not have met, standards of goodness against which you will be measured.

And the cure for shame, the treatment that lets you acknowledge your mistakes and grow from them, is Yom Kippur. We need Yom Kippur because we are fallible human beings. If we were machines, we wouldn't need a Day of Atonement. All we would need would be an annual maintenance, make sure our batteries were charged, check for rust and corrosion, tighten a few joints, and we'd be all set. If we were animals, without the burden of a knowledge of good and evil, we wouldn't need a Day of Atonement either. One day would be like any other. We wouldn't understand the notion that we had fallen short. But because we are human, we hear the voice that says, "You could have done better: you didn't have to do that." And again there is something deficient in our humanity if we don't hear that voice.

How does Yom Kippur neutralize that sense of inadequacy? This is the day when we drop our defenses, stop rationalizing, and admit our failures. "*Ashamnu, bagadnu, gazainu.* We have been selfish, we have misled, we have been greedy." And the message comes back from God: "Yes, I know that, and you're still acceptable in My sight."

HAROLD S. KUSHNER

You know, our Jewish people, God bless them, love their synagogues, but they have a limited capacity for organized worship. So instead of coming at the beginning of a long service and getting restless halfway through, we figure out when the service will be over, calculate back how much davening we can handle, and that's when we show up. Only once all year do we make an effort to get to shul on time, and that's tonight, for Kol Nidre. And it's the hardest service to come on time to. You have to leave work early, shower, get dressed, eat a big meal that will last you for twenty-six hours, park two blocks away, and try to arrive before the Cantor starts. Why do we do this? We don't understand it consciously, but at some level we need to hear Kol Nidre. Even if we don't understand the words, we need that message that the failures and mistakes of the past year won't be held against us.

And even before Kol Nidre, the opening words of the service are: "*beyishiva shel ma'alah uviyeshiva shel mattah anu mattirim l'hitpallel im ha-avaryanim,* the authorities in Heaven and on earth permit sinners to be part of the congregation." Why does the Mahzor begin the service with those words? Because it realizes that a synagogue that admitted only perfect people would be like a hospital that admitted only healthy people. It might be a lot more pleasant place but that's not what we're in business for.

Yom Kippur compels us to admit that "we are not machines; we get tired, we get distracted, just as Kasparov did in the chess match. We do bad things because we're angry or frightened or confused. And on our good days, we feel so bad about those things." And on Yom Kippur, God is pictured as saying, "That's all right. I don't expect you to be perfect." You know the Hassidic saying "Better a sinner who knows that he's a sinner than a saint who knows that he's a saint." God says, "I want you to know that there is forgiveness in the world. I don't expect perfection. I expect improvement. I expect wholeness. I want you to bring Me your whole self. Don't deny parts of yourself because you're ashamed of them, because you think they are less admirable than the rest of you. Don't try to hide parts of yourself from Me because you're afraid I won't like you if I saw the whole you. Bring Me your entire self, flaws and all, and let Me give you the sustaining message that your whole self is acceptable in My sight."

The pride of a machine is that it doesn't make mistakes. It performs as it was designed to. The glory of a human being is that we can make mistakes because so much is demanded of us, because what we aspire to be is so challenging. We can feel ashamed of our mistakes because we know there are such things as right and wrong, and we can grow from the experience, and from the discovery that there *is* forgiveness in the world.

And one more thing we do that machines, even the most marvelous of computers, can't do. Machines can't say No! Machines can't get angry and protest on moral grounds. They can't understand that some things are wrong. If I drive my car irresponsibly, my car will do all the dangerous things I tell it to do. My computer knows how to say "invalid command" but it doesn't know how to say "No, I'm not going to print that letter; it would hurt somebody's feelings." The glory of a human being, the most human, the most God-like thing we do, is often our ability to say No, to say No to things that tempt us but we know are wrong, and to protest, to say No to injustice, to corruption, to cruelty and immorality. When people who have been caught doing terrible things, whether in wartime or in business dealing, try to excuse themselves by saying, "I was only following orders," what they are admitting is that there is something lacking in their humanity. Machines obey commands; human beings, having tasted the fruit of the knowledge of Good and Evil, have the power and the obligation to pass those commands through the filter of their own conscience, their own sense of right and wrong.

What angers us about the behavior of the Swiss government in World War II was that, when they were asked to cooperate with evil, they couldn't say No. We would have expected more from fellow human beings. And what disappoints us about the behavior of the Swiss government today is that, when they were confronted with the evidence of what happened fifty years ago, they lacked the humanity to face up to what their predecessors had done. They had no sense of Yom Kippur, no room in their souls for a "holiday of regrets" to cleanse their stained souls. They could not say, as so many people cannot say, but as we are called on to say over and over on Yom Kippur, "We did wrong. We said Yes when we should have said No and No when we should have said Yes. We looked away to avoid seeing evil instead of standing up to it."

It has been suggested that you can measure the size of a person's soul by the size of the things he or she gets angry about. The Talmud says you can learn a lot about a person by the way he eats and drinks, the way he spends money, and the things that get him angry. When I was rabbi of this congregation, it was fascinating to see what got people upset. Machines, because they are soulless, never get angry. Small-souled people get angry over trivial things, the person who drives too slowly in front of them, the waitress who gets their order wrong. Other people, with more developed souls, would get angry over the fact that people go hungry in this country where we throw so much food away, that politicians take wealthy people more seriously than they take ordinary people. The burden and the glory of being human is to know that there things that are wrong in the world, and instead of our waiting for God to set them right, God is waiting for us to do it. This is the Jewish concept of the messianic hope, that what is wrong with the world need not be permanent, and that what ought to be one day will be, if only we can bring ourselves to be upset about what is wrong and enthusiastic about fashioning what is right.

I admit I was rooting for Kasparov to beat Deep Blue. I was rooting for

God's creature to defeat Man's invention, but I'm not sorry that the machine won, because it clarified for me what it really means to be human:

-that I can open my soul to joy, to love, to hope, and if necessary, to pain;

-that I can make mistakes, I can do wrong things, and still be acceptable to God and to those who love me, and I recognize my humanity in my willingness to be embarrassed by those mistakes;

-that as a moral agent, I can recognize things that are wrong and do something about them, *I'takken olam b'malchut shaddai*, to mend the world and fashion it into a world fit for God's rule.

THE MISSING PIECE

In Memory of Aaron Zev Kushner

1963–1977

Though we are all gathered in the same place at the same time for Yom Kippur, each of us comes with his own very personal agenda, his own hopes, dreams, fears, hurts, memories. I guess that's always the case when a large number of people congregate, but especially today, when the setting calls forth so many deeply personal responses. The prayer book tries to pull us together, by asking us to share the same words, but it's not really enough.

The prayer book tries to get us talking about sin and repentance, about cleansing and atonement. But our hearts resist. We don't respond to sin, to atonement. We want to pray about the verity of life, the pain of death and loss, the sustaining power of memory. And so strong are we in our insistence, in the gravitational pull we exercise on the service, that it finally has to accommodate us. When we open the Torah on Yom Kippur, to study the ancient rituals of purification, the opening

271

words deal not with Yom Kippur but with life and death: "The Lord spoke to Moses after the death of the two songs of Aaron the High Priest," as if the Torah itself had to concede that it can't begin to talk of atonement and cleansing until it has spoken of grief and bereavement first, because that is where our hearts are.

Let me begin by telling you a story, a strange kind of story that can best be described as a children's story for grownups. It was written by a man named Shel Silverstein and it's called *The Missing Piece.*

Once upon a time, there was a circle that was missing a piece and it was very unhappy. It went all over the world looking for its missing piece—over hills and across rivers, up mountains and down into valleys, through rain and snow and blistering sun, it went looking for its missing piece. And wherever it went, because it was missing a piece, it had to go very slowly. So as it went along, it stopped to look at the flowers and talk to the butterflies. It stopped to rest in the cool grass. Sometimes it passed a snail, and sometimes the snail passed it. And wherever it went, it kept looking for its missing piece.

But it couldn't find it. Some pieces were too big and some were too small; some were too square and some were too pointy. None of them fit. Then suddenly one day, it found a piece that seemed to fit perfectly. The circle was whole again; nothing was missing. It took the piece into itself and started to roll away. And now, because it was a whole unbroken circle, it could roll much faster. And so it rolled quickly throughout the world, past the lakes and past the forest, too fast to get a good look at them. It rolled too quickly to notice the flowers, too fast for any of the insects to fly by and talk to it. And when the circle realized that it was rolling too fast to do any of the things it had been doing for years, it stopped. It very reluctantly put down its missing piece, and it rolled slowly away, heading out into the world, looking for its missing piece.

Now that's such a beautiful story, I almost didn't want to spoil it, to violate its poignancy, by taking it apart and trying to understand it. But it's saying some important things. And the most important thing it is saying is that, in a strange, mysterious way that we can't really understand, a person is more whole when he's incomplete, when he's missing something. That little bit of incompleteness cures him of his illusion of self-sufficiency, opens him up—as it did to the circle in the story—to feeling more, seeing more, experiencing more. In a paradoxical way, the man who has everything will never have some of the most poignantly beautiful experiences in life. The man who has everything will never know what it feels like to yearn, to hope. He'll never understand the songs and poetry that are born out of longing, out of grieving, out of incompleteness. You can never make him happy by giving him something he would enjoy, because by definition, he already has it. In a strange way, the person who has everything, who is missing absolutely nothing, is a very poor person indeed.

We're more complete if we're incomplete. That's the paradoxical truth of the story. We are made more whole by the thing we don't have. I think that's true at many levels. When it comes to giving charity, we become more whole through what we give away. I think we instinctively understand that the person who can afford to be more generous, who can afford it psychologically, not only financially, is a more whole person than the man who is afraid to part with what he has, because he's afraid that if he gives something away, he's giving away part of himself. The wealthy man who needs to be asked three times before he gives, and thanked three times afterword, strikes us as, in some ways, an incomplete person; he may have a lot of money but he's lacking something more important. The man who is not afraid to be generous, because he knows he is not giving his self away, comes across as really more whole.

It is perhaps indicative of the culture we live in that many of us are familiar with the parables of the Fish and the Loaves from the New Testament—how a whole crowd of people were miraculous fed with just two fishes and several loaves of bread—but we don't know that the story originally comes from the Hebrew Bible, where it's told about the prophet Elisha.

V'ish ba miBaal Shalisha vayavey l'ish HaElohim lechem bikkurim v'carmel,

A man came to Elisha with a present of a loaf of bread and an ear of corn. And the prophet told him, "Distribute it to the entire crowd!" The man said, "What! Am I supposed to divide this among a hundred people?" And the prophet told him, "Distribute it to all the people for the Lord has said, It will suffice." And he gave it to them, and they ate, and left some over, as the Lord had promised. (2 Kings 4:42-44)

It's a nice trick to know when you have unexpected company. But the real point of the story is a more profound one. Each of us has the resources—the financial and emotional resources—to help a whole lot of people, but we don't know how much we have until we start giving it away. It's a scary thing, I can tell you from my experiences as a rabbi, to have people make emotional demands on you, to have them ask you to give them strength. That's why it's so much easier to find people to work with machines, with numbers, with pieces of paper, and so much harder to find people who can work with people. You're afraid that if you give them strength, you'll be left weak. But in fact, it works just the other way. The act of strengthening others makes you even stronger. The process of giving away leaves you more complete for having done it, like the pitcher of wine in Greek mythology that grew magically more and more full as people tried to empty it. You never know how rich and full you are till you start sharing yourself with others.

The person who has grown comfortable with the fact that he's missing a piece is, in a sense, more whole than the person who thinks he has to be complete, unbroken. When someone you love has died, there is no replacing that person. His death leaves an emptiness that will never be filled. A husband or wife can remarry and be very happy, a son can invest more of himself in his own family, a grieving parent in her remaining children. But whatever you do, you will go through life with a piece of you missing. No matter how full, no matter how crowded your life may go on to become, there will always be that empty space.

But the person who has survived bereavement (and that's all you can ever do with it, survive; you can't prevent it or undo it or ignore it)—the person who has survived and learned that losing part of yourself is an inevitable part of life—has become a more complete person than he could ever have been before. Nothing can scare him because he have been through the worst, and come through it.

I think the person I feel the closest to in all the pages of the bible is a man whose name I don't even know. All I know about him is one poem he wrote twenty-eight hundred years ago, Psalm 30, *Mizmor Shir Hannukat HaBayit.* We recite this psalm every morning at the beginning of the service and after we've said it, if there is a minyan present, the mourners say Kaddish.

Psalm 30 is the story of a man who used to believe that nothing bad could ever happen to him. "*V'ani amarti b'shalvi bale mot l'olam,* I once thought, while at ease, nothing could shake my security." And he was profoundly and sincerely grateful to God for being so good to him. In exchange, the man lived a moral life, prayed regularly, and gave to charity. Then suddenly, a series of terrible calamities befell him. "*Histarta panecha, havyiti nivhal,* You turned your face from me, and I was terrified." His whole world threatened to fall apart.

But then he made a vital discovery. He learned something about himself he could never have known before—that he was capable of believing in God and in God's world even when tragedy happened to him instead of to strangers. Before that, he could never have been sure of the quality of his faith. Did he serve God because He was God, or because God was good to him? Now he knows what he could have only hoped before, that there is nothing tentative, nothing conditional or self-centered about his faith. In a sense, God has given him something he never had before, the strength to go on despite his wounds, despite his sorrow. That's a great thing for God to give him; how could he have found his way without it?

In that same mysterious way of which we have spoken, there was something whole about his faith now, where it was immature and incomplete before. Missing a piece has somehow made him whole. The religion of "I love You as long as you're good to me" has been replaced by "I love you because You're God and because without You, I couldn't have made it."

It's not only a bereavement that forces us to go through that profound growth. Every one of us, in one way or another, is missing a piece. Every one of us has come to here an incomplete, unfulfilled person in one way or another. Some of us have been left incomplete by death, some by a divorce—a part of ourselves has moved out of our lives and somewhere out there, somebody is walking around with some of our most intimate memories; others of us, by a disappointment, the job we wanted and didn't get, the talent that would have made us so happy that we somehow never managed to develop, the child who didn't turn out as we hoped he would. Every one of us is incomplete in one way or another. We're missing something from our lives, and its absence weighs us down, slows us down (like the circle in the story), compels us to see everything in our lives a little bit differently.

Yet I would insist that we're made more whole by the experience of missing something, missing out on something. We learn reality, we come to see a world as it really is. The world isn't a birthday party, where if you've been good, everything happens the way you want it to. It's a very mixed-up unpredictable place, where hours of sunshine alternate with hours of darkness, redeemed by occasional flashes of bravery and love.

We learn gratitude; precisely because we can't have everything, we learn to be grateful for what we do have. Children don't understand that. For them, the world is divided into what they have and what they don't have yet but intend to have. The idea that there are some things they won't ever have, and that some of the things they have may be taken away from them—that's hard for them to understand. And probably that's just as well. They deserve a few years to be children: they'll be wise long enough. But we who roll through life slowly, with our missing pieces—we understand that.

In the Grace after Meals, there is a line toward the end: "May God bless me and those around me as He blessed Abraham, Isaac and Jacob, *biv'racha shlemah*, with a complete blessing, with everything, a blessing from which nothing is lacking." And the Midrash, the commentary, notes, "Maybe Abraham, Isaac, and Jacob were blessed by God with a *bracha shlemah*, a blessing from which nothing was missing. But nobody since then has been."

And in fact, when you think about it, Abraham, Isaac, and Jacob had their missing pieces as well. They had problems with their parents, their wives, their children. Abraham broke with his father over a matter of religion, left him, and never saw him again. He sent one of his wives out of his house into the desert. He had a son who intermarried and caused him grief.

Isaac was almost killed by his father as a child. When he grew old, he lived with his wife and children but had nothing to say to them. They were living in opposite directions, they had forgotten how to trust one another.

Jacob ran away from home as a teenager. He quarreled with his father, with his brother, with his father-in-law, and he saw his sons quarrel viciously with each other. And they came as close as anyone in the Bible to receiving a bracha shlemah, a complete blessing with nothing missing.

The fact of the matter is, there is no such thing as a life that isn't missing a piece. It can't be a full life without disappointment, without pain, without loss. Maybe that's what the prayer really means when it says that Abraham, Isaac, and Jacob received a complete blessing. Maybe it doesn't mean that they got everything they wanted and kept it. Maybe it means that God have them a *full* life, a life full of love and full of pain (because how can there be love without pain?), a life full of hope and full of disappointments (because if you hope grandly enough, you'll have your share of disappointments). Maybe instead of giving them an easy life, God gave them a full life, a bracha shlemah, a blessing of fullness, a life full of joy and full of ears, full of accomplishments and full of failure. And we ask that God give us that kind of fullness, that kind of wholeness too.

To be missing a piece, to have to go through life carrying around an emptiness where something important and precious to you used to be, and to understand despite the pain that you are a deeper and richer person because you're missing that piece—that's what it means to be whole. That Hassidic master, the Kotzker Rebbe, used to say, "There is nothing in all the world as whole as a broken heart," and sooner or later in this life, each of us comes to understand what he meant.

The Torah makes the same point. In the opening lines of the Book of Leviticus, when it speaks of how our forefathers used to worship God with animal offerings, it says "*adam ki yakriv,* When a man brings a sacrifice …" Several times for each of the categories of offering, it repeats those words, "adam ki yakriv, When a man brings a sacrifice …" Then, when it comes to the very last kind of offering, the mincha, the poor man's offering, it suddenly changes the wording, and now it says "*nefesh ki takriv,* When a soul brings a sacrifice …"

The commentators respond to the change of language; what kind of sacrifice does a soul bring? This is their answer: Sometimes there is something you want very badly, to the very depths of your soul. You work for it, you pray for it, you say to yourself and to God that if you could only have that, you'd be happy, you wouldn't want anything else. But one day you have to acknowledge that it's not going to come your way, like Moses at the end of the Torah, realizing that he's never going to reach the goal he has spent his life working for. If you can do that without losing your soul, without becoming so embittered that life will have no further meaning for you, if you can be like the circle at the end of the story, if you can let go of your missing piece and roll away to face life without it, that's nefesh ki takriv. That's the sacrifice of one's soul that we bring and lay on God's altar, and turn away, feeling whole in a way that we could never feel whole before.

Proof